Anonymous Anonymous

The Angel Guide

Anonymous Anonymous

The Angel Guide

ISBN/EAN: 9783744659505

Printed in Europe, USA, Canada, Australia, Japan

Cover: Foto ©Thomas Meinert / pixelio.de

More available books at **www.hansebooks.com**

THE

ANGEL GUIDE;

— OR —

YEAR OF THE FIRST COMMUNION,

TRANSLATED FROM THE FRENCH

BY

CHILD OF MARY.

The Original has been approved by the Bishops of
Perpignan and Bayeux.

———o———

MONTREAL :
PRINTED BY JOHN LOVELL & SON.

Dedication.

St. Michael's Palace,
Toronto, March 17th, 1885.

We earnestly recommend to the good children of our Archdiocese a small book entitled "The Angel Guide," or "Year of First Communion.

The reading of it will strengthen to persevere in the good resolutions and purposes made at First Communion.

†JOHN JOSEPH LYNCH.
Archbp. of Toronto.

Imprimatur,
Marianopoli, 13th Sept , 1885.
† EDUARDUS,
Car. Episc. Marionopolitamus

O my Good Angel, defend me!

THE ANGEL GUARDIAN.

FROM THE GERMAN.

To each sweet child, so young and small,
  God sends an angel guide,
In lowly hut or castle hall,
  Each little step beside:
Thus ever guarding night and day
With tender care its feeble way.

God doth command this angel kind
  To watch this tiny child,
And both his body and his soul
  To shield from dangers wild.
True to his trust, the angel stays
And watches o'er its youthful days.

And when the mother's anxious heart
  With tender grief is riven,
The angel takes her tearful prayer,
  And wafts it up to heaven.
O happy mother, happy child!
He guards them both, this angel mild.

THE ANGEL GUIDE ;

-or-

YEAR OF THE FIRST COMMUNION.

1st January, 1880.

MY dear child, the year has at length arrived in which you will have the happiness of receiving your FIRST COMMUNION.

That you may be well prepared is the sincere desire of my heart, and for this reason I wish you a very happy New Year.

Listen attentively, my child, and follow with eagerness the paternal advices that I will give you on this subject.

In the first place, be fully penetrated with this great truth, that your FIRST COMMUNION, my beloved child, will exercise a great influence over your whole life, and, consequently, that this year is for you a most important one, since upon it may depend your whole future; for the FIRST COMMUNION, worthily or unworthily received, may decide your happiness or unhappiness, not only for time but for eternity.

Oh, Father! you have almost frightened me; tell me, I pray you, what is necessary for me to do that I may receive worthily, and that my Communion may be a foretaste of an eternity of happiness. Mark out to me all the prayers you wish me to say, and I promise to say them regularly.

Prayers, my child, however good, are not here so essential; religious instruction and a truly Christian spirit are much more necessary.

You can plainly see how many children err upon this matter. However, as you seem to have an attraction for prayer and other exercises of piety, I shall furnish you with some.

Place your FIRST COMMUNION, my dear child, under the special protection of the Blessed Virgin, of your Angel Guardian, and of your dear Patron.

Recite, every day after your morning and evening prayers, a Hail Mary, to ask of God through the intercession of the Blessed Virgin the grace to Communicate worthily, to which you may add the following invocations :

God the Father, my Creator,
God the Son, my Redeemer,
God the Holy Ghost, my Sanctifier,
Holy Trinity and one only God,
} Grant me the grace to receive worthily my First Communion.

Holy Mary,
Holy Angel Guardian,
Holy Patrons (N. and N.),
St. Louis of Gonzaga,
St. Stanislaus of Kotska,
St. Philomène,
St. Virginia,
St. Rose,
Blessed Imelda, patroness of First Communicants,
All ye Angels and Saints of Paradise,
} Pray for me, that I may worthily receive my First Communion.

Lamb of God who takest away the sins of the world, Spare me, O Lord.

Lamb of God who takest away the sins of the world, Hear me, O Lord.

Lamb of God who takest away the sins of
the world, Have mercy upon me, O Lord.

Christ hear me.

Christ graciously hear me.

Well now, my child, do you think that you
can say these prayers regularly every day?

Yes, Father, I promise you.

Then, my child, you are seriously determined to receive worthily your FIRST COM-
MUNION?

Yes, Father.

The next most essential thing for you to
do, is to study to know yourself, so that you
may correct your bad habits, and replace them
with the contrary virtues. Do you understand?

Not very well, Father.

Well, then, listen to me attentively while
I explain. Can you tell me what you know
of the good or evil that is lurking in your
heart?

O, dear Father, there are many things that
I would not like to tell you.

If I were your Confessor, my child, you
would have to tell me all, but as I am only
your Mentor, or Angel Guide, there are many

things relative to conscience of which I need not be made acquainted, and which can be but little treated except in the holy tribunal; these I will only point out, without asking you about them, and I do not wish you to tell me those things even should you desire it. No I assure you, it is only that you may know how to explain things to your Confessor, and they should be the first you should tell, but, remember, to him you must tell all; and if you wish me to direct you well, except on this point, you must tell me the rest.

Let us return now to the first question: tell me, except those things that belong to the confessional, all that you know of good or evil in you.

But I do not understand, Father, what you would wish me to say.

How, my child! Do you not every day do something naughty as well as good? Is there not in you what we call good and bad traits, vices and virtues?

Ah! I now begin to understand, Father, you no doubt speak to me of my anger, gluttony, idleness and disobedience. Is it not so?

Precisely, my child, and of many other

things besides. But is there nothing but wickedness in you; is there not some good; tell me in all simplicity and without self-love?

Ah, Father, self-love, that is one of my defects, my parents and teachers have always told me.

So much the worse, my child, but can you not find some virtue?

Very little, Father.

It is a great pity, my child, the virtues are so essential. At least have you not compassion for the poor?

Yes, I am sorry for them, and I give them occasionally some little alms.

Well, my child, this is the virtue that we call *charity*, but is this the only one in your heart?

I believe so.

Examine yourself again: when you see your parents sick or afflicted does it not give you pain?

Oh yes, very much indeed.

Well this is at least another virtue, which we call *filial affection*; and now is there nothing in your heart for God?

O yes! I love Him and I pray to Him from time to time.

Very well, that is the third virtue, which we call *religion.* Now you see, my child, by little and little, I shall teach you to know yourself, that is, to know all the good or evil that is in you, so that you may correct the evil, and perfect the good, and thus acquire those virtues that are wanting, for I repeat it: this is the principal preparation for your FIRST COMMUNION. Do you understand now?

Yes, a little, Father.

I shall not insist on any more for to-day; you will come to me in fifteen days; until then, you will have plenty of time to reflect upon what I have told you of the *good* and *evil* that you have already discovered, so that you may know yourself more and more. Continue to find out still more what good and evil you possess, and come and tell me in all simplicity and confidence, so that, knowing you better, I can direct you more easily. In the mean time begin your principal preparation for your FIRST COMMUNION, by diminishing or correcting entirely, your *anger, gluttony, idleness* and *disobedience,* of which you have spoken, and increasing those heaven-born gifts of *charity, filial piety* and *reli-*

gion. Now, remember, I shall examine you well.

So much the better, Father, that is what I wish, because in thus questioning and examining me, you teach me many things that I did not know before.

Now, my child, I recommend you at this happy time, preparing for your FIRST COM-MUNION, to go to confession at least every month; and now, remember to say regularly your morning and evening prayers.

To go to Mass and Vespers every Sunday and Holiday of obligation.

To assist regularly at Catechism.

Never to eat meat on Friday.

To respect your parents and superiors.

To fly from bad company.

To be careful never to tell a lie, and to avoid the occasions of sin; above all never to sing or listen to bad songs or to uncharitable discourses. In a word, apply yourself to correct all your failings, and specially your predominant one, and pray to your blessed Mother that you may know it.

In passing thus the first month you will have begun to make an excellent preparation for your First Communion, and God will bless you.

Farewell, my dear child; on the fifteenth do not forget to come to see me.

I shall not forget, dear Father.

JANUARY 15TH.

FATHER, I have come to tell you some of the good and some of the evil to which I am inclined.

Above all, my child, give me an account of your behavior since the fifteenth?

Won't it do after?

No, my child, begin by that.

Well I have been some better.

That is too vague, you must give me more details. Upon what points have you improved? and in what have you failed?

O! Father, that is too hard!

It is for your good, my child.

I know that.

Well, then, begin.

I have been less impatient and less angry, and less disobedient, too;—but for gluttony there is very little change, and for idleness, I think I have conquered a little.

Well, my child, thank God for your first victories, and humble yourself for the new faults you have committed; apply yourself during the rest of this month to correct more and more your impatience and disobedience; fight against your appetite, and do your utmost to overcome idleness. But, my child, it is not only necessary to correct your faults, you must do good and practise virtue in order to receive worthily your First Communion. Tell me what good you have done and what virtues you have practised since New Year's day?

O! Father, I cannot say.

Think a little, my child; this is only the second time—you remember those virtues of which I reminded you, *charity*, *religion* and *filial piety*, which were budding in your heart, can it be possible that since that time you have not made acts of those virtues?

O yes, I say my prayers every morning and evening, unless when I am too lazy to get up, and I give my heart to God on awaking, and also before I go to sleep, I also gave some alms to a poor person the other day, and when Papa was sick I took care of him.

Well, my child, always remember to say your prayers regularly, and give your heart to God night and morning. Now, my child, you see the good and the evil which you have still discovered in yourself.

Father, I do not know how it is that I find out the evil quicker than the good. Besides my anger, disobedience and gluttony, I tell lies sometimes, and Mamma says my predominant passion is being too headstrong.

Oh, my child, you must apply yourself to correct those faults, in order to receive worthily our dear Lord. But tell me, now, do you not play too much?

Yes, Father, I do.

Now, you must only take moderate recreation. Are you not inclined to be sulky, jealous?

Sometimes.

Well, these are other faults to correct, and now, do you not take things that do not belong to you?

Oh! no.

Not from any person, not from your parents?

No, Father.

So much the better, it is an ugly fault, and children who are inclined to it should correct themselves before they receive their FIRST COMMUNION. Tell me now, my child, of the good which you have discovered in yourself.

I have sought and I cannot find any, unless the virtues you have already spoken of, *religion, charity* and *filial piety ;* only people sometimes tell me I have a good heart."

Well, this does not seem reconcileable with the bad disposition of which you have spoken a while ago. Can you remember upon what occasion that was said ?

Father, when I get angry, and when the passion is over I entertain no ill-will, and I speak just as usual, and would do those who injure me a service when I can, even if I know them to entertain ill-will against me ; when I see even an animal suffering it grieves me, and I would not wish to injure any one whatsoever.

Effectually, my child, you have a good heart, or I should say there is in you a great mixture of good and evil, which proves the proverb, 'That the good and the evil never go alone, and in the most wicked heart there is always something good, as in the best there is something bad.' But let us see, in a good heart there are other qualities : when you have done any thing wrong, are you sorry for it ?

Yes, Father, I am.

Do you love to make others do wrong ?

No, Father ; is it possible that there are hearts wicked enough for that ?

Yes, my child, and they must correct that if they wish to receive worthily their FIRST COMMUNION.

I wish, my child, to enter into those details that you may know yourself, and I now repeat it, the principal preparation for your First Communion consists in correcting your faults, and cultivating those virtues which are already in your heart. This is what is called being wise.

O Father, I thank you ; no one ever spoke to me of that before.

That is, my child, because you had not arrived at the period of your FIRST COMMUNION.

Very well, my child, come the first of February, I have other things to teach you which will surprise you more. Farewell, dear child ; go and reflect upon those two conferences of the 1st and 15th of January.

FEBRUARY 1ST.

HAVE you been faithful, my child, to all that I recommended to you on the first day of the New Year relating to your FIRST COMMUNION?

Yes, dear Father.

Have you said your morning and evening prayers, a Hail Mary after your prayers?

Yes, Father.

And have you been to Mass, Vespers, Catechism and Confession?

Yes, Father.

Have you eaten meat on Friday?

No, Father.

Have you sung bad songs, or read bad books?

No, Father.

Very well, my child. God be praised! I begin to think you will be well prepared for your FIRST COMMUNION.

Now, we come to the essential point. Generally speaking, children who are preparing for their First Communion, say their prayers and do what they are ordered to do; they also acquit themselves of their religious duties, but do they correct their faults and thus become truly wise ?

Now, my child, how are you with regard to your faults ?

Father, I have corrected some of them, but others I have not.

Which faults have you corrected ?

Being lazy and telling lies.

Courage, my child, that is a great deal.

And now what are the faults which you have not corrected ?

Impatience, rash judgments and disobedience. I could not help it.

Well, my child, that is the effect of long habit, and it requires grace and all the efforts of your will to overcome these vices; but hope in God and the grace of our Lord Jesus Christ. This time, your report is quite contrary to the one you made the last time ; because then you had triumphed in a great measure over your impatience and disobedience, and you had fallen again into gluttony and idleness ; now, you have overcome gluttony and idleness, and have fallen into impatience and disobedience; and, to excuse yourself, say that you could not help it ; rather say, my child, that you have not made the same efforts against those bad habits; and conclude that, with the grace of God, and your own will, you can certainly correct those passions; do you not think so, my child?

Father, I promise to make stronger efforts to overcome those faults, and I hope the next time, Almighty God will be satisfied with me.

You need not be surprised, my child, if you still fall into impatience, disobedience and rash judgments; they are difficult to correct, because they come from contradicted pride and self-will, but we must oppose pride and self-will, this is what we call overcoming one's self; have you not sometimes conquered yourself?

Sometimes, but more frequently I have been conquered.

Well, have courage, one cannot succeed all at once; you have already gained many victories, which proves that it is possible to accomplish a complete victory. It is well to distinguish what is deliberate and voluntary from what is not deliberate or wilful; the first impulse of anger may overcome; but it is no sin, unless the will takes a part in it. A false judgment or a curse may surprise you by the force of habit, but it can be retracted, and, if you renounce it at once, there is no sin. But for disobedience, listen: " A father," said Our Lord Jesus Christ, "had two sons ; he said to one ' go there;' ' I go not,' responded he, but, having repented his fault, he went; the father said to the other : ' go there,' ' I go,' said he, and he did not go." Which of them did the will of his father ? Evidently the first. This example proves that the first movement of disobedience can be repaired by after-submission. Begin, then, by renouncing your bad habits of anger, cursing, rash judgments and disobedience, and firmly resolve to correct them.

O, dear Father, now I understand; and I promise to make every effort to overcome those temptations.

Well, my child, you have come now to the acquiring of virtue. What virtues have you practised ?

Really, Father, I think I have not practised any.

But, my child, the victories you have gained over impatience and disobedience are certainly produced by the contrary virtues,

mildness and obedience ; whilst idleness, gluttony and telling untruths, are corrected by the
virtues of diligence, temperance and sincerity,
which are beginning to blossom in your heart.
Once more, my child, have confidence ; be sure
that God has been pleased with you under all
these circumstances, and that, even here, He
will reward you for those acts of virtue which
He has seen you practise, and He will prepare
great consolations for you on the day of your
holy FIRST COMMUNION. Praying to God
night and morning are so many acts of religion;
learn, then, to know what is good in you as
what is evil. Have you not given some little
alms ?

Oh yes, Father.

See, these are acts of *charity.* Think if you
cannot find out some other virtue.

Father, I have been sometimes sick, and I
offered my sufferings to our dear Lord to
expiate my sins; is that a virtue ?

Without doubt, my child. There are two
virtues, the spirit of penance, and the virtue of
resignation. Think again, my child ?

Well, Father, when I am scolded instead
of being headstrong and murmuring, I some-

times say to myself, you are to blame, and you just deserve all that was said.

Very well, my child, this is the virtue of *submission*, and also of *humility*. All will go well, my child; continue, and you will have no faults, but all virtues, when you will make your FIRST COMMUNION.

Father, you told me to-day that you would tell me things that would astonish me.

It is true, my child, but I have not time; come on the fifteenth, and I shall tell you. I have to-day one other advice to give you.

ADVICE.

You understand the necessity of correcting your faults and bad habits, and replacing them with the contrary virtues, do you not, my child?

Yes, Father.

You remember that I told you there are passions, and following these passions are faults, that we only speak of before God, and in the holy tribunal of penance. Well, my child, these faults are against the Sixth Commandment, that is, against modesty. Listen to me, then, without saying anything; profit according to your wants before God of what I am going to tell you.

I listen, Father.

Know, then, my child, that any one who is unhappily prone to such habits and passions, should speak to his (or her) Confessor, as you have come to speak to me of your other faults, to learn how to correct them. For this sin is the most terrible, the most culpable, and the most opposed to the sanctity of the Holy Communion. A child who is a slave to those habits should necessarily correct them, and acquire the opposite virtue of modesty, without which he will certainly make a sacrilegious FIRST COMMUNION. Now, my child, console yourself, for, I trust, by the grace of God, you are not in this pitiable state ; but, as it sometimes happens that children whom you would not suspect are slaves to this horrible vice, I thought it necessary, to ensure your salvation and a happy FIRST COMMUNION, to give you such advice, for the better understanding of which read the examination of conscience under the Sixth Commandment. After reading this, you will understand why I have wished you to read it ; and I would advise you, at the foot of the Cross, if you have anything to reproach yourself on this point, to ask forgiveness; and if you are still in happy innocence, let not the reading of this afflict you. Let us return, now, to your FIRST COMMUNION. In five months, my child, you will make the Holy Communion, oh, the happy day which will unite you to Jesus in the Blessed Sacrament! Increase your fervor as the time approaches; continue what you have done in the preceding month, but strive to become better and better. A feast of the Blessed Virgin occurs during the month, that of the Purification of the Most Blessed Virgin, which falls on the second of February: say one decade of your Rosary every night, and assist, if possible, at Mass every Saturday, in honor of the Mother of God, that, through her intercession, you may obtain the grace of receiving worthily your FIRST COMMUNION.

IMPORTANT ADMONITION.

On Shrove Tuesday, do not give yourself up to those foolish amusements which are so common, and, if the Forty Hours is established in your Parish, follow religiously the exercises,

to counter-balance the levity of the world.
On Ash Wednesday, receive the ashes in the
spirit of penance, and in remembrance of
death, which blights the fairest flower, as well
as the sturdy oak; accustom yourself to little
mortifications at your meals, to expiate the
faults of gluttony to which you have been
addicted; observe faithfully the rules of your
Parish with regard to the use of flesh meat.

Go, my child, and may God bless you!
come to see me on the 15th.

Yes, Father. Adieu! I recommend myself
to your prayers.

And, dear child, remember me in yours.

FEBRUARY 15TH.

" God of Mercy, Truth and Right,
Give Thy ransomed children light,
Here His sacred law to prize
And to see Him in the skies.

TO-DAY, my child, our thoughts must
turn to great subjects; listen attentively
and answer me.

Do you believe in God, my child?

Yes, Father, why do you ask me that?

Do you believe that you have a soul?

Yes, Father.

Do you believe in heaven and hell?

Yes, father, I believe certainly, but why do you ask me these questions?

Do you believe in the eternity of heaven and hell?

Yes, Father, I believe in life everlasting, it is the last article of the Creed. But why ask me these questions?"

I wish by these words: GOD, HEAVEN, SOUL, ETERNITY, and by the truths they express, to prove that most men are blind and insensible, and that, perhaps you yourself have been so until now, and to tell you again in what *wisdom* or virtue consists, in order to receive worthily your FIRST COMMUNION.

This is a lesson in philosophy that I give you, my child. I do not intend to do less than make you a philosopher, and a great philosopher.

True philosophy consists in the practice of wisdom and in living conformably to religious belief, when it is a well-founded belief as yours is. Now then, my child, you say you believe in GOD, SOUL, HEAVEN and ETERNITY; very well, let us make here a JUST BALANCE that of faith, and even simple reason; place GOD on one side and the *world* on the other, and weigh them :—on one side put your SOUL and on the other your *body*, and weigh them ; on one side put HEAVEN and on the other *earth*, and weigh them ; on one side put ETERNITY, on the other *time*, and weigh them.   Is it not evident that GOD is infinitely above the *world* ? is it not evident that your SOUL is more precious than your *body?*   Is it not evident that the *earth* is as nothing when compared to HEAVEN ?   Is it not evident that *time* is nothing when compared to ETERITY ?   What do you think, my little philosopher ?

It is true, Father.

Then the true philosopher, that is, the wise man who seeks true happiness, must always prefer GOD to the *world*, but never the *world* before GOD ; always the SOUL to the *body*, and never the *body* to the SOUL ; always sacrifice *earth* to HEAVEN and never HEAVEN to *earth*, always *time* to ETERNITY, but never ETERNITY to *time*.   How are your thoughts now, my little philosopher ?

It is true, Father.

But it is not what men do.   Slaves of the *world*, they sacrifice GOD and their RELIGION slaves of their *body*, they sacrifice their SOUL and their happiness ; slaves of the *earth*, they sacrifice HEAVEN ; slaves of *time*, they sacrifice, ETERNITY. Is it not true, my child ?

Yes, Father, it is too true.

How blind and insensible do they not become ?

Evidently so, dear Father.

But, my child, what have you done until now.

Like them, dear Father, I have had little thought of God, and have had only the world in view. I took great care of my body, and I almost forgot my soul. I occupied myself with earth, and I did nothing, or almost nothing, for heaven—a slave of time I forgot eternity.

And now having learned this philosophy what do you think of persons that act thus ?

That they are blind and foolish.

And, my child, since you wish to be a true philosopher, what must you do ?

Just the reverse of what I have hitherto done, that is, serve God above all, even if I should lose the whole world ; take more care of my soul than my body ; sacrifice always earth

to heaven, never heaven to earth; time to
eternity, and never eternity- to time.

Such, my child, is true wisdom, the only
true philosophy; do this and you will be a phil.
osopher and a great philosopher; do it, and you
will have made the first and principal preparation for your First Communion; do it, and you
will thereby practise all those things of which I
have spoken to you in the previous entertain--
ment. You will correct all your defects and
acquire all the virtues, for whosoever, in all
thing prefers, GOD to the *world*, the SOUL to
the *body*, ETERNITY to *time*, has no longer any
defects, he has only virtues ; at least, his
defects disappear more and more each day,
while his virtues, in the same degree, are per-
fected.

Consider, my child, the great things which
I had to teach you to-day, and be no longer
surprised that I addressed to you those four
questions.

Oh, dear Father ! you have done me a
great service; you have opened my eyes to-day
to great and new thoughts, my mind to things
that I never reflected upon.

You now see the truth of the words of the

Holy Ghost : Leave the thoughts of thy childhood and live a new life, walking in the path of wisdom ; and in those days I will give you a new heart and a new soul."

But why, Father, did you not tell me these things before ?

My child, you have heard them before, but you did not seem to comprehend. Now, this new heart, this new soul, is given you by God before you approach your FIRST HOLY COMMUNION. Go, my child, and from this day until the first of March, meditate frequently on these four great words, GOD, SOUL, HEAVEN, ETERNITY; weigh them continually in the balance of faith with those other words, the *world*, the *body, earth* and *time ;* and be forever a true philosopher.

Yes, Father, during the remainder of my life I shall keep in my heart these four words : God, Soul, Heaven, Eternity, or at least the truths they contain ; and shall endeavor to reduce them to practice, as a preparation for my First Holy Communion, so that during the rest of my life I shall follow the path that you are opening before me.

B

MARCH 1ST.

DEAR Father, you see me here again, this is the first of March.

That is well, my child; your promptitude is admirable. Well, now, how have you passed the second month of the year of your First Communion?

Not badly.

You mean to say well, I hope.

Have you said your decade of the Rosary every evening, my child?

Yes, Father.

And heard Mass every Saturday?

Yes, Father. I assisted also on Thursday it being consecrated to the Holy Sacrament, and I thought in assisting at Mass on that day it would be a good preparation for my First Communion.

Very well, my child, think seriously, you have but four months to prepare to receive our dear Lord in the Holy Communion. Try and pass those four months as you did the first two, in the exercise of piety; on the 25th, the day of the Annunciation, ask, through the intercession of the Blessed Virgin, the grace to perform well this holy action for which you are preparing. Every day recite the following prayer:

PRAYER WHEN PREPARING FOR FIRST COMMUNION.

O divine Jesus! I shall soon for the first time receive into my poor heart Thy adorable Body and Blood, Thy soul and Thy divinity; the happy day is fast approaching—the happiest of my life, because, oh dear Lord! Thou lovest children, but above all, those who receive Thee with innocent and pure hearts. Oh Adorable Jesus! give me the grace to preserve this precious innocence, if I already possess it, and if I have the misfortune to have lost it, restore it to me through Thy gracious mercy and my sincere repentance, so that I shall receive Thee on the day of my FIRST COMMUNION with a pure heart, experiencing the divine and tender caresses with which Thou didst favor little children, during the days of Thy mortal life. O! may I merit like them to be blessed with that paternal benediction that will accompany me all my life, and be for me the pledge of eternal happiness in the Home of my Father. Amen.

RECOMMENDATIONS.

Before the month closes, and in the following one, you will celebrate the mysteries of Our
Lord's Passion, of His Resurrection and of His
Ascension; listen to what I shall tell you. At
the service of Holy Thursday, think how our
Lord instituted the Holy Eucharist, the first of
all the Communions given by His own hands.
I told you at the beginning of the year, my
child, how you should receive your FIRST COM-
MUNION, upon which might depend your eternity. Now, you will see I was not deceiving
you; twelve Apostles for the first time received
from our own dear Lord's hands the Holy
Communion; eleven received well; one, the
unfortunate Judas, received badly; and the day
after he fell into despair, hanged himself, and
is now in hell; the eleven others are saints
reigning with God in happiness. Think upon
this, my child, and tremble, but have also hope,
for God is good, and with this double influence
of fear and confidence, prepare yourself more
and more for so decisive an action. On Good
Friday, the day our dear Lord died on Calvary,
go to the foot of the Cross and adore Jesus
crucified for love of you; kiss the sacred

wounds of His feet, hands and side ; weep, my child, because the faults of your childhood have been the cause of His death. On Holy Saturday, the day our Lord remained in the tomb, go and prostrate yourself at the foot of the holy sepulchre, and ask again pardon of Jesus for the faults of your first years which have crucified Him. On Easter Sunday, celebrate the glorious Resurrection of Jesus Christ, rise spiritually with Him, and rejoice to think that next year you will receive your first Easter Communion on that great day. Now, my child, these are recommendations that I give you—you see that I count a good deal upon your piety and good will ; engrave them on your memory. You may now go, but go in peace ; pray to Jesus and Mary to bless you.

Do not forget to come back soon.

When, Father ?

To-morrow, if you wish. I told you on the 1st of January, the third preparation for the FIRST COMMUNION was religious instruction, to which subject I promised to return. I hope I shall be able, so come to-morrow."

Yes, Father.

Adieu, pray for me.

MARCH 2ND.

FATHER, you promised to explain to me the third preparation for the FIRST COMMUNION, religious instruction.

It is true, my child. But do you remember well the first two preparations?

Yes, Father, to correct my faults, and to practise the contrary virtues, that is, to prefer God to the world, my soul to my body, heaven to earth, and time to eternity. Beside this, I must practise my religious duties, which include my prayers.

That is very good, my child, but you must, above all, know your Catechism, not merely the words from memory, but you must try also to understand it, and firmly to believe all the truths explained to you, that you may live according to the doctrines of Jesus Christ. There are children that only retain in their memory the words of the Catechism, and far from believing its truths, do not even understand them, and consequently do not put them in practice ; these are unfortunate children, But for you, dear child, who have had so many advantages, apply youself more than ever to

an intelligent and practical study of your
Catechism, that is to say, your religion, of which
it is the abridged explanation.

Besides these four great truths which we
considered the last time—the existence of
God, the spirituality and immortality of the
soul, the future life and the eternal duration
of its punishments and rewards; besides these
four first and fundamental truths, do you
believe in original sin ?

Yes, Father.

Do you believe in Jesus Christ, and in the
mystery of His Incarnation and Redemption ?

Yes, Father.

Do you believe in the Holy Gospel, the
Christian Religion, and the Holy Catholic
Church established by Jesus Christ ?

Yes, Father.

Do you believe in the *grace* of Jesus Christ,
and its necessity for our salvation ?

Yes, Father.

Do you believe in the seven sacraments,
and particularly Confession and Holy Eucharist ?

Yes, Father.

Do you believe in the commandments of God, and the Church?

Yes, Father.

Do you especially believe the obligation of observing the Lord's day, and that of fasting and abstinence?

Yes, Father.

Do you believe in the Holy Sacrifice of the Mass?

Yes, Father.

Do you believe in death? I mean death considered according to faith. Do you believe in the private judgment after death, in the resurrection, and the general judgment?

Yes, Father, I believe.

All these truths, my child, and others are contained in the Catechism; but what effect have they had upon your mind and heart? How do they influence your conduct? Acknowledge that until now they have been, for the most part, words without any meaning, like those other four great words—GOD, HEAVEN, SOUL, ETERNITY, which you had learned and repeated hundreds of times without having understood them, but now, meditated and understood, what a light beams

upon your mind ! what new impulses in your
heart ! and what an admirable reformation in
your conduct ! so far even, we might say, as
to change all your defects into virtues ! So
shall it be, my child, with these new words :
*Original Sin, Redemption, Incarnation,
Jesus Christ, Cross, Gospel, Christian Religion, Catholic Church, Actual Sin, Grace,
Sacraments, Baptism, Penance, Eucharist,
Sacrifice of the Mass, Commandments, Sunday, Fast, Abstinence, Easter Duty, Death,
Particular Judgment, Purgatory, Hell,
Resurrection from the Dead, General Judgment.* So shall it be, I say, with these words
if you will take account of them, and meditate upon them as you did upon the four first
words I gave you ; you will find in them new
light for your mind, new sentiments for your
heart, and new rules for your conduct, that
will make you stronger in the path of wisdom ;
that is to say, you will be enabled the better
to correct your vices and bad habits, and perfect your virtues. This will be a holy preparation for your FIRST COMMUNION. In reflect-
ing upon these other words, *Original Sin,
Incarnation,* &c., you will become not only a

philosopher, but a Christian philosopher, a true
disciple of Jesus Christ, and you will understand why you go to confession and communion, why you hear Mass on Sunday, why you
do not eat meat on Friday, in a word, why you
accomplish all your religious duties which are
so much mocked at by the world, and far from
blushing at your religious practices you will
glory in them.

There, my child, is the grounds of all the
explanations which have been given you at
Catechism; but, alas! giddy as you were, you
perhaps only seized the words, this is what we
call the letter of the Catechism.   Once more,
endeavor from this time till your FIRST COM-
MUNION to take in the spirit of the Catechism;
and you will see that all things are linked
together in the religion of Jesus Christ, and
that when you have laid hold of one ring of
the chain, you must soon relax your hold, or
draw on the whole chain; there is no middle
course.

I would like to know what progress you
have made in overcoming your bad habits, and
in practising virtue, but I have already kept
you too long; come in a few days again.   In
the mean time, expect a serious examination.

March 8th.

TO-DAY, my child, I wish you to give me an exact account of your principal preparation for your FIRST COMMUNION—I mean as regards the reformation of your defects, and the acquiring of virtues.

Alas, Father! it is always this that embarrasses me most.

What do you wish, child? The more trouble the more merit. Begin quickly; it is always your self-love that holds you back.

It is true, Father.

No doubt, my child, it is humiliating to tell your faults; you would rather have only virtues, were you actuated by the love of God, and not the love of yourself—

Ah, Father, you understand me perfectly, but I will tell you all. I have told one lie, been gluttonous twice, disobeyed once, and been in a passion three times, but without cursing.

Is that all?

Oh, Father! it is too much, when I think that it is only three months till I shall receive my FIRST COMMUNION.

It is true, my child, you should desire to be an angel, but, at the beginning of the year you had a great many bad habits, and already there is a great change for the better. I truly admire what the grace of God has done in you, while also feeling sad that you have been led into other faults. I admire still more the victories which grace has enabled you to gain; for is it not true, that, without grace and the efforts of your own good will, you would have committed many other faults?

Oh yes, Father, is it true. It seems to me that there is a demon always pushing me on to do evil; I have the greatest trouble to resist him.

Without doubt, my child, we have all of us a wicked angel about us, urging us to offend God, but we have also our Guardian Angel, who encourages us to do good, and inspires us with good thoughts? Have you not sometimes seemed to hear him say to you on the part of God just the contrary of what the devil suggests?

Yes, Father, because when I am tempted to do evil there is always a voice which says, 'do not do it', and when I resist the temptation another voice says, 'why do you not do it,' so that I always hear the two voices, and two different inclinations at the same time, one pushing me on to do good, and the other to do evil. What is the cause of that, dear Father ?

My child, that is what we call the combat of nature and grace : these are the two opposing powers of which St. Paul speaks, the contradiction between our souls and our bodies; sin consists in yielding to nature and the devil, and virtue in following the inspirations of grace and the counsels of our good angel, who will lead us to God.

In another instruction, I shall teach you my child, how to combat with the devil. Cheer up, and be not discouraged. Let us speak now of the virtues that you have practised in preparing for your FIRST COMMUNION.

Father, I have thought of sometimes eating dry bread for my breakfast in punishment for my sins.

Did you do so?

Yes, Father.

Very well, this is the virtue of *penance*. What else have you done ?

Three times in passing a Church, I have gone in to salute our dear Lord, whom I shall soon receive in the Blessed Sacrament.

Continue my child, this practice, sometimes it will bring great blessings upon you;
this is the virtue we call *piety*. What else
my child?

One day I was very much inclined to
anger, because one of my companions teased
me, so I went away entirely from him, lest I
should swear or say something wicked.

That is the virtue, my child, which we call
prudence. But have you not a little vanity
or self-love?

Yes, Father, I am glad you spoke of that.

Because you think that I esteem you, is it
not?

Yes, father.

Well, my child, this is *vanity*, and you
must forget me, and rejoice only before GOD
for doing good, then avoiding vanity, which
is a defect, you will practise a new virtue,
purity of intention, which consists in having only GOD in view, and desiring only to
please Him in the good that we do, and the
virtues we practise. But tell me, my child,
about your being headstrong, sulky, &c. Are
you still inclined to those faults?

Sometimes, a little.

Well, my child, correct that little, too, so that you may become more and more agreeable to God, and thus ensure a good FIRST COMMUNION. Now, come and see me again on the first of April.

Yes, Father. Please give me your blessing, that God may give me His grace.

The blessing of God be with you, in the name of the Father, and of the Son, and of the Holy Ghost. Amen.

APRIL 8TH.

WHY, dear child, what has been the matter. I have been quite anxious about you ; you are very much altered, have you been sick ?

Yes, Father, and I feared I should have died before receiving my FIRST COMMUNION.

Well, if there was any danger, you could have received Holy Communion in your bed, it would have been a great happiness ; for a child who, on the bed of death, receives worthily, goes to heaven, and there is always a fear that you might not persevere in virtue.

Oh, dear Father, I hope I shall be always wise, and always love God.

I hope so, dear child, but what about your sickness ? You might have died, many children die before receiving their FIRST COMMUNION, and some on the very day receive their first and last, which we call the Viaticum. Think well, my child, and do all that you can as if you were to die in the night of that happiest of days.

I wish I could, for I do love our dear Lord with all my heart, and I would be very happy to go with Him to Heaven.

Now, my child, as you are suffering, I shall not detain you long, nor shall I overcharge you with work, suffice it to say, that, as the happy day approaches, you should become better and better, the more worthily to receive and then to entertain our dear Lord ; during the month, go twice to confession, assist at the Holy Sacrifice two or three times a week, if your parents consent ; instead of one decade, say two of your Rosary. Go, my child, take care of your health, but more especially of your soul.

Farewell, Father. When shall return ?

In eight days, when I must teach you how to overcome the temptations of the devil, the enemy of your salvation.

APRIL 12TH.

BUT, my child, you have come very much later than I told you to come. I am too busy to speak to you to-day; go and do just as your little head teaches you, sometimes too soon and sometimes too late, not as I tell you at all. When you correct yourself of those whims, I shall speak with you.

Forgive me, dear Father; it was not the fault of my will, I assure you, but——

Oh, I see; you wish to excuse yourself; this little self-love that cannot bear the least word. Go, I told you to go, and come another time.

When, dear Father, shall I come?

I have already said ix eight days.

Farewell, dear Father; pray for me; I am much in need.

My child, come here. You believed I was angry with you?

No, Father, but you are so busy, and really I must be importuning you?

No, dear child, you do not importune me; it was a little trial I wished to give you to understand you better, and see where you are in regard to your old defects. My child, you have just now practised several virtues, *sweetness, resignation, humility,* and *obedience.* Before now, you would have answered me impolitely, you would have been sulky, and perhaps have determined not to come back again. What has caused this change? The grace of God alone working in the heart, when it meditates on these four words : GOD, SOUL, HEAVEN, ETERNITY. Remember, my child, always to act thus when you are contradicted, and you will be a faithful imitator of Jesus Christ in His sweetness, His patience, and His humility.

Now, what have you done, my child? tell me confidentially. I see you have some sorrow. I wish to comfort you. What? you weep? Is it because I have scolded you a little? This self-love must be corrected.

Oh no, Father, it is not that, but you have been so kind, and treated me with such, goodness.

Well, my child, there is another good trait in your heart—*gratitude*—another virtue. Now tell me, as to your father, all your sorrows.

Father, I came earlier than you desired me, having for some days past been very much tempted by the devil, and you promised to show me the way to resist and overcome him. I thought I had better come and see you, for I was afraid that I should yield.

You have done well, my child. · I am sure it was your Angel Guardian that directed your steps to me. If you had not come you might have committed some great sin, and what might have been the consequence?

Always act thus, my child, and never wait until you have fallen into sin; whenever you find the temptations are strong, and the devil wishes to enchain you, go and confess these temptations, and the tempter will fly. God will bless you, and the grace of the sacrament will sustain you. This is the principal way of combating the devil, but I shall give you other means.

How to Combat the Temptation of the Devil.

When you are tempted, my child, always make the sign of the Cross; you can do it secretly if you are in company, just make it upon your heart, and pronounce the names of Jesus and Mary, from which the devils fly. Repeat the sixth request of the Lord's prayer, "lead us not into temptation, but deliver us from evil." At other times you may speak to the devil in the words of Jesus Christ himself when the angel of darkness dared to tempt Him. Our dear Lord spoke to him these words: *"Thou shalt not tempt the Lord thy God. Man lives not by bread alone, but by every word that proceedeth from the mouth of God. Retire, Satan; it is written the Lord thy God thou shalt adore, and Him only shalt thou serve."* To these words, which caused the devil to fly, is attached a particular grace. Another means of avoiding sin, is to place yourself at the foot of the Cross, regard with compassion the sorrowful spectacle—Jesus dying for love of you. But, above all, my child, avoid the occasions of sin, never entertain bad thoughts, call your Angel Guardian to your assistance, for God has given him charge to bear you up lest you fall into sin; pronounce these great words: GOD, SOUL, HEAVEN, ETERNITY! In a word, keep yourself united to God, and pray to Him in the secret of your heart during all the time the temptation lasts, and should that be all your life, you will never fall. The devil can do nothing against those who have not the will to yield to him.

Say, now my child, what have become of your temptations, while I have been speaking to you ?

Oh, Father, I have no longer any. I am quite calm.

Return thanks to God, my child. You see that a pious conversation may dispel the most violent temptations. Profit by the experience, and you can scoff at the devil. Go in peace, and come to see me on the first of May, for I shall have many things to say to you. It is the month of our dear Mother Mary, through whose powerful intercession, I hope you will obtain the grace to receive worthily our dear Lord for the first time into your heart. This will be the last month of preparation for your FIRST COMMUNION.

MAY.

FATHER, this is the first of May, and you
told me to come on the first.

Yes, my child, I remember, for, as I told
you, it is the last month, preceding the one of
your FIRST COMMUNION, and you should render
it more holy than all the others. Besides, it is
the month of Mary, the month of our dear
Mother. Sanctify, then, this lovely month,
which is especially consecrated to her, adorn
her statutes with the flowers of May, but, above
all, dear child, cultivate the virtues which
will beautify and adorn your heart, that heart
which so soon will be the altar upon which
Jesus will repose.

PRAYER FOR A CHILD PREPARING FOR FIRST COMMUNION TO REPEAT EVERY DAY.

O Mary, Mother of God and Mother of men,
behold at thy feet one of thy children, who
desires, in preparation for his First Holy Communion to celebrate worthily the month consecrated to thee. Bless me, dear Mother, and
increase my fervor that I may bedeck my heart,
soon to become the Altar of Jesus, with the
virtues of purity, humility and obedience.

Obtain for me, O Mary, a tender love for Him, who for the first time I shall receive into my heart, and whom thou didst carry for nine months in thy chaste womb. Amen.

RECOMMENDATION.

During this month go to Mass every morning, if possible ; read some pious book every day, for at least a quarter of an hour, on the subject of Holy Communion, and at night do not fail to say your Rosary, because the great day is fast approaching, my child, and you cannot be too well prepared.

At the beginning of this month you will be examined on your Catechism, in order to ascertain if you are sufficiently instructed to Communicate. Pray to God, my child, that He may enlighten those who will decide, but resign yourself to that decision. Ask with great fervor that you may not be received if you should be so unfortunate as to be ill-prepared for your FIRST COMMUNION. Do you understand, my child?

Yes, Father, I shall do so to-day, for to-morrow we shall be examined.

To-morrow, well, I shall say nothing more

to-day, go now and prepare yourself for your examination, and submit to it cheerfully; when it is over, come and let me know the result. If you be sent back, I shall put off for another year the advices which I have still to give you.

MAY 2ND.

I can see, my dear child, by the expression of joy in your countenance that you have been received for your FIRST COMMUNION. Have all the children who are attending Catechism been received ?

No, Father, seven are retarded until next year. Father, some of them were very angry, and said they would never come back to Catechism again; and others cried a great deal, but said they would prepare themselves better next year, and they asked us to pray for them.

Now you see, my child, the first of these were not prepared, and Almighty God did not permit them to be received; the second were better disposed, and I am sure will do their utmost next year. Pray for them, but at the present occupy yourself entirely with your own duties.

GENERAL CONFESSION.

Now that you are received, my child, for your FIRST COMMUNION, you must begin your General Confession, that is, a full confession of all the faults which you have committed since the use of reason, as if you had never confessed them. You will devote to it the whole month. You must divide your confession into four parts, taking one each week.

Firstly. Examine yourself on the first three Commandments of God, and confess.

Secondly. On the following three.

Thirdly. On the rest of the Commandments of God, and those of the Church.

Fourthly. On the seven deadly sins, and the duties of your state of life.

Now, my child, I wish you to recite the following prayer before each of your examinations:

PRAYER BEFORE EAXMINATION OF CONSCIENCE.

Behold me, oh my God, a guilty child that I am; since the age of reason I have often and grievously offended Thee by thoughts, words, deeds and omissions. Alas! I cannot remember the number nor the circumstances of my sins; long since have they been buried in mist and darkness. Thou, O God of goodness! hast established in Thy Church the Sacrament of Penance for the remission of the sins committed after Baptism; but it behoves me to make a serious examination of my conscience if I desire to avoid being judged and condemned by Thee for the sins of my childhood. Suffer me, O Lord! to judge and condemn myself at Thy holy Tribunal, by a sincere and humble confession, that I may hear from the lips of Thy minister those sweet words, "depart in peace, thy sins are forgiven thee." Assist me, O God of Wisdom! that I may know my sinfulness, dispel the darkness that surrounds me, and, with the brightness of Thy light, show me the malice and enormity of my offences, so that I may confess my sins and sincerely detest them.

O Mary! assist me to discover my faults.

Holy Angel Guardian, and my holy Patron pray for me.

After this prayer, examine yourself upon the Commandments of God.

First Week or Entertainment.

Of General Confession.

I. *Commandment.*

I am the Lord thy God, thou shalt not have strange
gods before me.

On Faith.—Father, I accuse myself of being
negligent in learning the truths of Religion ;
of having wilfully doubted of articles of faith
(tell what article) ; of having listened to and
said things against God, Religion, and persons
consecrated to God ; of having read books
against Religion ; of having acted through
human respect, been ashamed of making the
sign of the cross, or kneeling down to pray ;
mocked those who seemed pious.

On Hope.—Father, I accuse myself of having
sinned, by presuming on the goodness of God
to offend Him with greater liberty ; of having
committed many times the same fault, saying
I can confess them all together, other times
wanting confidence in God by despairing to
receive pardon or securing my salvation, or
that I should be able to reform my bad habits ;
of having delayed my conversion, saying, I am

not going to die soon; of murmuring against God in my sorrows and troubles; of saying that God was not just to give me more than my share of trouble.

On Charity.—I accuse myself of not loving God; of thinking seldom of Him; of having resisted His inspirations, and of following the suggestions of the devil; of seldom offering my actions to God, and doing nothing for His glory or His love.

On Religion.—Father I accuse myself of not giving my heart to God on awaking; of not saying my morning and evening prayers; of having abridged them, and said them without attention or devotion, in bed, or without kneeling, talking or listening to others talking during prayer; of not being recollected in church, laughing at religious objects; consulted fortune-tellers; believing in lucky and unlucky days; giving credence to dreams.

IMPORTANT ADVICE.

It is thus, my child, that you will confess yourself of each and every one of the commandments; but, remark, that it is not necessary to repeat, Father, I accuse myself, at eac

sin—it would lengthen uselessly your confession, you will only say it before the principal
sin of each commandment.

Secondly. You should not accuse yourself
of all the faults that are spoken of in each
commandment, but only those of which you
are guilty.

Thirdly. You must respond in all sincerity
to the questions proposed by your Confessor.

Now, my child, that you may not be forced
into a formula of examination, but that you
will examine yourself, I shall vary continually the following commandments, giving
them sometimes one way, and sometimes
another, and you must examine yourself and
confess accordingly. The First Commandment
will serve as a rule for all the others.

II. Commandment of God.

Thou shalt not take the name of the Lord thy God,
in vain.

A child sins against this commandment when
he affirms what he says by the holy name of
God ; or when he swears to a falsehood, which
is perjury; when he swears he will do some-

thing he has no intention of doing ; and when he will not do that which he has sworn to do, if it be in his power; when he says, *may God punish me if it is not true—that I may never live—as true as there is a God, &c., &c.;* when he forces his companions to raise their hands and swear ; when he blasphemes, which is to speak ill of God and his saints ; when he uses the holy name of God with impious and bad words ; when he makes imprecations against himself or against his companions, against animate, or inanimate objects ; when he does not accomplish the vows which he has made to God or the Blessed Virgin. He should not pronounce the holy name of Jesus and Mary uselessly or without respect.

Now, my Child, examine which of those faults you have committed, and confess them in this form : Father, I accuse myself of having, &c. Tell first those sins which you consider mortal, the circumstances which aggravate them and the number of times committed, each has been. Continue this with all the Commandments. Now, do not forget, for I shall not repeat it again.

III. Commandment of God.

Remember that thou keep holy the Sabbath day.

To this command may be added the 1st precept of the Church : To hear mass on Sundays and Holydays of obligation.

You have sinned against the Third Commandment if, since the age of reason, you have not assisted at Mass on Sundays and Holydays of obligation—the age of reason is generally supposed to be about the age of seven years—if you came too late for the sacrifice—or if you were present only in body, that is, without attention or devotion ;—if again, unable to be present, you did not recite some prayers in order to sanctify that part of the day. Have you prevented your comrades from going to Mass ? Have you neglected going to Vespers, or did you fail to perform some act of religion to sanctify the afternoon of the Lord's Day ? Did you work on Sunday or cause others to work? There are certain journeys opposed to the sanctification of the Sunday, also certain trading.

Confess if you were late for Mass, and if you lost a considerable part of it, also if you have worked on Sunday, how long, and at what kind of work ?

Do not examine yourself any further to-day, but go to confession after having recited the prayers for making a good confession,

Second Week of Instructions for the General Confession,

Having recited the preparatory prayer, page 57, for the examination of conscience, see if you have not forgotten any faults which come under the first three Commandments, or if, since your last confession, you have not committed some other sins,

IV. Commandment of God.

Honor thy Father and thy Mother.

The principal faults of a child of your age, are not to love his parents, to hate them, to murmur against them, to speak ill of them, to mock them, to wish them evil or their death, to be wanting in the respect due to them, to be angry with them, to disobey them, to not pray for them during life or after death.

In after years you can examine if you have attended to their wants during their old age

or sickness, and particularly at their death—
if you have procured for them the last Sacraments, and accomplished their last will. See
also, if you have not committed similar faults
against your grandparents, uncles and aunts, or
against your superiors. Other faults against
this Commandment are, to hate your brothers
and sisters, argue with or ill-treat them, have
them punished unjustly, refuse to be reconciled with them, not to salute or speak to them.

To despise the poor, servants or old people,
treat servants unkindly ; to scold them un-
necessarily.

V. Commandment of God.

Thou shalt not kill.

A child may commit homicide by injuring
his neighbor in four different ways.

First, *in his body.*—By ill-using or strik-
ing his companions, by exciting them to
quarrel ; he also sins by injuring himself in
any way, either by excess or violence, or wishing his own death ; lastly and worst, by com-
mitting suicide.

Second, *in his soul.*—By bad advice ; bad
example, scandal, seducing other children.

C

Third, *in his heart.*—By bearing him hatred, by wishing him evil and even death, also by rejoicing at the misfortunes of others, by refusing to pardon or salute them, by giving them trouble, or causing them unhappiness.

Fourth, *in his honor.*—By injurious language, false reports, rash judgments and suspicions.

Particular note on this Commandment.

Retract all calumnies. Pardon those who have offended you, and if you are at variance with any one be reconciled.

VI. Commandment of God.

Thou shalt not commit adultery.

Examine yourself upon these faults. Bad thoughts, bad desires, immodest looks or actions, keeping indecent statues and pictures, speaking bad words, listening to unchaste discourses, singing or reading unchaste songs, reading romances or other bad books, lending them to others, indecent plays, dangerous friendships, especially between children of different sexes, immodest postures, scandalous balls and dances, immodest dress, or carelessness in the act of dressing or undressing, exposing one's self immodestly, taking pleasure in thinking over bad dreams.

ADVICE.

' If, my child, you have committed or fear to have committed, any other faults which are not here expressed, do not fear to confess them, no matter how wicked they are, or what shame they may occasion you; if you do not know how to explain them, ask the assistance of your confessor, or, if your confessor thinks it necessary to ask you questions, do not be embarrassed, but respond in all sincerity and simplicity of heart. If you do not understand his question, do not trouble yourself, tell him candidly, Father, I do not understand you, and continue your confession, so as not to delay any longer your companions.

Particular note on this Commandment.

You must quit bad company, burn or destroy all bad books, and unchaste songs, also immodest statues and pictures.

Do not examine yourself any more to-day but go to confession, after having recited the prayer to make a good confession at page 76.

THIRD WEEK OF INSTRUCTION FOR GENERAL CONFESSION.

Recite as in page 57 the prayer of preparation ; examine, then, with care, if you have not forgotten some sin under the three preceding commandments, also what faults you have committed since your last confession.

VII. And X Commandments of God.

Thou shalt not steal. Thou shalt not covet thy neighbor's goods.

Have you stolen from your parents or other persons money, fruit or other objects, from your companions, books, paper, pens, etc. Have you encouraged others to do so ? Have you cheated at play, or in buying or selling ? Have you paid all your little debts ? Have you given to the proper owners things that you found ? Have you tried to find out to whom they belonged ? Have you given away things without your parents' consent ? Have you broken, injured or lost by your fault what belonged to your parents or others ? Have you killed or maliciously wounded domestic animals ? Have you taken money from the poor ? Have you torn or destroyed your clothing to obtain new garments? Have you neglected the care of things given into your charge? Have you received stolen goods, or kept them for others.

Remarks particular to this commandment.

It is often necessary to tell the quality and quantity of the things stolen, or objects destroyed or lost.

It is not only necessary to tell the damage which is done, it must also be repaired as far as possible.

VIII. Commandment of God.

Thou shalt not bear false witness against thy neighbor.

Officious lies or lies told in fun are generally but venial sins; they might sometimes be mortal, when they are averred by an oath. Wicked lies that would cause a person to lose his place, his practice, or his prospects, false testimony, opening the letters of others, reading secret papers, revealing the secrets of others which are expected to be kept conscientiously.

Particular note on this Commandment.

You are obliged to retract all lies which injure your neighbor, and also to repair any injury you have done him as far as in your power.

COMMANDMENTS OR PRECEPTS OF THE CHURCH.

The First Commandment is contained in the Third Commandment of God.

Second Commandment of the Church.

To fast and abstain on the Days commanded.

This commandment enjoins on us to fast on the days commanded by the Church.

The commandment of fasting will be obligatory on you only when you will have attained the age of twenty-one years. Then you will examine if you have fasted every day in Lent except Sunday, every Wednesday, Friday and Saturday of the Quarter tenses or Ember days ; also the eve of great Feasts, such as Christmas, Easter, Pentecost, and the Wednesdays and Fridays of Advent (if such is the usage in your diocese). In case you were lawfully dispensed, you should supply by other penances for the fast or otherwise by prayers or alms.

For the present, examine if you have eaten between meals on fasting days, without necessity ;—or eaten meat on Friday, or other days, on which it is forbidden.

Third Commandment of the Church.

To confess our sins at least once a year.

A child sins against this commandment when, arrived at the age of reason, he does not confess, but waits till the age of eight, nine or ten years to make his first confession :—when afterwards he does not confess at least once a year ; when he does not examine his conscience sufficiently, nor prepare himself for confession ; when he has not contrition for his sins, nor purpose of amendment, or tells lies in confession ; when he does not perform his penance, or performs it badly ; when he does not accomplish the promises exacted of him by his Confessor; when he does not restore ill-gotten goods ; when he despises the advice given him, or subjects his Confessor to ridicule ; when he asks his comrades what was said to them at confession ; or when he tries to hear the confession of others.

Note. If a child had the misfortune to conceal or disguise a sin in confession, it is not enough simply to tell it the next time he goes to confession; he must accuse himself positively of having concealed or disguised it.

Fourth Commandment of the Church.

To receive worthily the Blessed
Eucharist at Easter or within the
time appointed.

To be retarded from your FIRST COMMUNION
by your carelessness and indifference in learning your catechism; or by your want of piety
or wisdom; or having the intention of making
a bad Communion if you could, are grievous
faults, and should consequently be confessed.

The rest of the Commandment only regards
the time after your FIRST COMMUNION. Have
you communicated worthily at Easter, or how
often have you neglected your Easter duty?
Have you communicated without preparation,
without piety, without thanksgiving? with a
doubtful conscience, or positively guilty of
even one mortal sin? which would render your
Communion a sacrilege.

Fifth Commandment of the Church.

To contribute to the support of our Pastors.

Though, my child, this commandment of
contributing to the support of the clergy employed in your parish does not regard you at
present, you should take notice that it will be
hereafter as bounden a duty as the payment
of your rent or any other just debt.

Have you neglected to pay your pastor his just dues? If your means did not allow you to give even a small contribution, have you obtained a dispensation?

Sixth Commandment of the Church.

Not to solemnize marriage at the forbidden times, nor to marry persons within the forbidden degrees of kindred, or otherwise prohibited by the Church, nor clandestinely.

This precept, my child, may be passed over in your examination, as it does not regard a child of your age. Nevertheless, it is a very important law of the Church, and its non-observance is a grievous offense, and leads to great unhappiness.

Terminate this third examination by the prayer, page 76; then go to confession, observing what has been said to you before.

FOURTH WEEK OF INSTRUCTION.

OF THE GENERAL CONFESSION.

Recite the preparatory prayer before the ex-amination of conscience, as in page 57. See if you have not forgotten anything in your last confession, or what other faults you have committed.

CAPITAL SINS.

PRIDE.

Pride of Thought.—Self-love, vanity, good opinion of one's self, ambition, desire of praise of honors, pride of beauty, of voice, of figure, of clothes, &c.

Pride of Words.—Boasting of one's family, one's fortune, of one's talents; speaking of one's self to be admired.

Pride of Action.—To act for admiration, to be headstrong, self-conceited, and hypocritical.

Avarice.—Excessive love of money; immoderate desire to be rich; not giving to the poor; regretting what you have given.

Luxury.—Under the sixth Commandment of God.

Envy.—To be afflicted at the prosperity of others; envying their place, or talents; rejoicing over their sorrows and adversity; being jealous of brothers, sisters or companions, or of the praise given them.

Gluttony.—Eating or drinking too much; using immoderately intoxicating drinks; eating between meals without necessity, especially on fasting days.

Anger.—Impatience with others; quarrelling and disputing; furious conduct; angry with every one because contradicted.

Sloth.—Laziness in study, in work, in rising in the morning; losing time and making others lose it; never obeying promptly, always deferring.

DUTIES OF THE STATE OF LIFE.

Catechism. —Failing to be present; not learning your catechism, nor listening to the explanation; diverting the attention of your comrades.

School.—Absenting yourself from school through your fault or too great a desire of play; feigning illness; inducing others to stay away; losing your time; disobeying your teachers; not learning your lessons; not doing your duty, and thus having your parents to lose their money; clubbing together, exciting rebellion among the students.

Work.—Not doing your work, or doing it negligently; not sanctifying your work by offering it to God.

See now, my child, the prayer you should recite after each of your examinations of conscience.

PRAYER FOR THE FIRST COMMUNICANT TO EXCITE CONTRITION.

Behold, O my God! the numberless faults which I have committed against Thee. Alas! those which I have forgotten are perhaps more numerous still. O, how miserable am I, what an ungrateful and guilty child for having offended so good a God, so tender a Father! One of these sins, if it were mortal, is sufficient to merit hell. Alas! had I died after having committed it, I should now be among the reprobate, lost for all eternity! Oh! how many times already have I sacrificed heaven, how many times have I exposed myself to hell!...But what afflicts me most is that, by my sins, I have crucified anew Jesus Christ. O my divine Saviour! pardon me, I beseech Thee; give me, I conjure thee, a contrite and humble heart; make me weep bitterly over my sins, as Thou didst weep Thyself in the Garden of Olives. Make me to fear them more than death, and grant me Thy holy grace that I may rather die than to offend Thee mortally for the future.

Mary, refuge of sinners, pray for me.

Here, my child, take your crucifix, and

kiss the five wounds of your crucified Saviour. Would that your heart, rent with sorrow, might break forth in sighs; would that your eyes could be moistened with a few tears; at least, let God see your soul sorrowful, like that of Jesus Christ in the Garden of Olives when weeping and expiating our sins. He is good and merciful, the God that you have offended; He will be moved to compassion and will forgive you your sins.

Go, now, and cast yourself at the feet of the Priest to make your confession, but recite beforehand the following prayer :

Prayer before Confession.

It is at Thy feet, O my God! that I cast myself on entering this Holy Tribunal; it is to Thee I confess, in the person of the Priest, Thy minister; how useless for me to hide or disguise my faults. Thou hast seen me commit them, Thou knowest them better than I do myself. Do not permit, O my God! that shame or fear prevent me from declaring them ; put sincerity into my heart and truth upon my lips, and make me fully to understand that it is the sincere acknowledgment of my faults before this, thy earthly tribunal, which will secure thy merciful forgiveness; for what Father will refuse to pardon his guilty son when he accuses himself. Thy representative will also pardon me in Thy name. Like the prodigal child I come to Thee, O Heavenly Father! to acknowledge my transgressions, persuaded that Thou will pardon and receive me into Thy tender embraces. O my God! it is with this holy confidence that I cast myself at Thy feet. How easy is it for me to tell the greatest sins, when I think that it is to a Father who already desires to pardon and comfort the offender.

O Mary! refuge of sinful hearts, assist me by thy powerful protection.

O holy Angel Guardian! I have often afflicted you by my sins, come and I will console you by my sincere and humble confession.

Holy Patron, intercede for me that I may make a good confession.

ADVICE AND METHOD FOR CONFESSION.

On entering the Church go and adore Jesus Christ in the Adorable Sacrament of the Eucharist, and then salute His Blessed Mother recommending to her maternal care your confession; next take your place at the Holy Tribunal, following those who preceded you, without pushing, talking, or laughing; keep yourself modest and recollected, reading, praying, and examining your conscience, but, above all, exciting yourself to contrition.

On entering the Confessional, which you should do without noise, begin by making the sign of the Cross. Then say, Father, bless me, for I have sinned. Whilst the Priest gives you his blessing recite, with head inclined, the *confiteor*, until you come to the words " through my fault," at which you stop, then say, Firstly, how long since you were at confession. Secondly, if you received absolution or only benediction. Thirdly (after your-FIRST COMMUNION), if you went to Holy Communion. Fourthly, if you performed the penance given you. Then begin by telling the faults which you had forgotten or did not sufficiently explain, or perhaps concealed or disguised in your last Confession; continue by those which you have since committed, and then take up your general confession from the commandment at which you left off, saying,

Father, I accuse myself of having, &c. When you have confessed all your sins term'nate thus, *Father, I accuse myself of all the faults that I have forgotten, and all those of my past life. I humbly ask pardon of God, penance and absolution (or benediction) of you, my ghostly Father*, and finish your confession by saying, *Therefore I beseech*, &c. Listen attentively to what the Priest shall say, without examining if you have confessed well and without interrupting him ; answer his questions if he should make any, accept the penance he gives you, and, inclining your head, make an act of contrition whilst he pronounces the words of absolution or benediction. After having made the sign of the Cross, retire softly and modestly ; then at the feet of our Dear Lord Jesus recite the following prayer :

AFTER CONFESSION.

My God! How good art Thou! and how happy am I! Of what a burden has my heart been relieved! How consoling is confession ! Why did I fear it so much ? I thank Thee, O God ! for having given me the strength to accuse with sincerity all my faults. With the assistance of Thy holy grace, I will never more commit sin, and I shall avoid all the occasions of it. I shall follow the advices which have been just given me by my confessor, and I shall perform with exactitude the penance imposed upon me. O my God! how trifling it is compared to so many faults! how easily dost Thou pardon, O my God! but I shall not abuse of Thy goodness to offend Thee. I shall never more sin against Thee. No, never. I would rather die than offend Thee mortally for the time to come.

Recite your penance, and then if you have received absolution say the prayer at page 97. Do not leave the Church until you have at the Altar of Mary recommended yourself to her.

ADVICE.

The Confessor, on your leaving, recommends himself to your prayers, and you should indeed pray for him. I advise you to make it a practice, after confession, to recite one *Pater* and *Ave* for him who is guiding your soul, through the storms of life, to your eternal home.

There, my child, is all that I had to tell you

for the Month of May, that decisive month during which you will make your General Confession, which, good or bad, will determine a good or a bad FIRST COMMUNION. My child! my dear child! how often during this month shall I think of you. I promise to pray much to our good God for you, and to recommend you frequently to the Blessed Virgin. Do not forget to pray often yourself. Go, dear child, think that the great day is fast approaching—but come and see me on the first of June.

O, Father! do permit me to come before, at least once or twice during this month of May.

Very well, my child, come.

MAY 12TH.

First Return of the Child.

I would have come long before, Father, only I feared that you might have too much to do. Since I have begun to make my general confession, I have great anxiety.

What is the matter, my child?

Father, it appears to me that I shall never be able to tell all the sins of my life, and I fear that God will not pardon me.

O my child, what do you say ? God is good and merciful, and He has promised to pardon the most grievous sins, provided we confess and repent of them. Are you not in these dispositions, my child ?

Oh ! Father, if—

Very well, if you think God will not pardon you, you believe that He is not good, and that He will deceive you ?

Oh ! no, Father, no.

You now see, my child, that your fears are ill-founded, and these are what we call scruples.

But, Father, if I forget sins in my general confession ?

Even so, my child, no matter what care you may take, or how well you may examine yourself, you will always forget some, perhaps a good many, but God will pardon you all that you may forget without having the will, and that is why I told you to add at the end of your confession, *I accuse myself of all the sins which I have forgotten.* Now, child, do not worry yourself any more, do you promise me ?

Yes, Father, give me your blessing, and I will go in peace.

I bless you, my child, in the name of the Father, and of the Son, and of the Holy Ghost. Amen.

Thanks, Father, pray for me.　Adieu.

MAY 15TH.

Second Return of the Child.

YOU have come again, my child, and your eyes are red, as if you had been crying a good deal ; what is the matter ? Scruples again to make you sad ?

Oh Father, Father !

Well, what is all this ?

I fear I shall not be prepared for my FIRST COMMUNION, c perhaps I may not be able to go at all.

For what reason ?

Our Director sent back two of the children preparing, because he had heard of something very wicked which they had done, and he said they would communicate unworthily if he had not come to know it : and if he comes to know that I am so bad, he will not allow me to receive, lest I, too, might commit a sacrilege.

But, my child, all sins are not the same; probably those children are hypocrites. No matter how wicked you have been, have you not confessed your sins?

Yes, Father.

And you will never commit them again, nor offend God any more?

No, Father, I never shall.

Well my child, when your Director understands your life, and sees your good dispositions, he will, with joy and confidence, be the first to have you communicate, and your FIRST COMMUNION will be a happy one; calm yourself, my child, and go in peace. If these two unfortunate children of whom you speak were to correct their faults, like you, they would communicate worthily; see now, what it is not to confess and correct one's faults.

Oh, Father, thanks. I feel satisfied that I shall be well prepared for my FIRST COMMUNION.

Yes, my child, I sincerely hope so, but now do not return until 1st June.

MAY 25TH.

Third Return of the Child.

PARDON me, Father, if I trouble you again, but two of my companions who were received for their FIRST COMMUNION have been sent back by their Confessor after having made their General Confession. Alas! Father, what if my Confessor sends me back also?

And why, my child, why would he send you back? A Confessor will only send a child back for one of these three reasons: because the child has not the will to cease from sin, or because he does not repent; or perhaps he has concealed sins in confession, and his Confessor perceives it. Now, can you say that you are in any such sinful disposition?

Oh! no, Father, I have told them all, and I sincerely repent of having so much offended God, and I promise sincerely never to sin any more.

That will suffice, my child. I promise that your Confessor will give you absolution, and that your FIRST COMMUNION will be a good one.

Thanks; Father, I will not worry any more. I am quite happy. Adieu! Father, I will pray to God for you.

And I for you, dear child. Farewell.

JUNE 1ST.

MONTH OF THE FIRST COMMUNION.

BEHOLD, at last, my child, the beautiful month for which you have so long sighed, the month of your FIRST COMMUNION; rejoice in it, bless it, offer it to God. Of all the months of the year, let it be through life the first and dearest to your heart. The beginning of this month should be employed in preparation for your FIRST COMMUNION, and the end in acts of thanksgiving. I have no new practice to give you for this month. Spiritual advancement, as I have already said, does not consist in multiplying your devotions, but in trying to perform with greater fervor those which you have already practised, and laboring to correct the faults of your childhood, and to produce acts of the contrary virtues. Apply yourself, my child, during the few days that are given you:

Firstly—To correct more and more your old defects, vivacity, disobedience, gluttony, self-love, and particularly the faults which were the most profoundly imbedded in your heart, and which you had so much trouble to uproot, for even during the last month you have fallen into them several times, in spite of your resolutions and promises.

Secondly—Try and perfect more and more the virtues that you have begun to acquire, gentleness, modesty, humility, purity, obedience,—but especially humility and sweetness, for I see with sorrow, my dear child, that you still retain a great deal of pride and impatience. At the same time, I am not suprised, and do not be discouraged yourself, for bad habits are easily acquired and hard to overcome, while the virtues are slowly acquired, and very easily lost.

Thirdly—Be more exact in your exercises of piety, your prayers, spiritual reading and examinations. Alas! how many distractions have hitherto accompanied them! You are so giddy, is it not true that from time to time you have no devotion in your exercises of piety. Now then, my child, be more attentive.

and more pious during this month so precious
to you. Above all, I recommend you to assist
every day at the Holy Sacrifice of the Mass ;
be there the adoring angel but in spirit
and in truth,—do you understand, my child ?
for God, and not for those who see you, as
that would be only human, hypocritical piety.

The only additional exercise to which I
would exhort you is,—after prayer every
morning to spend seven or eight minutes in
meditation on Holy Communion, or, if the
Stations of the Cross are erected in your
Parish, perform this devotion sometimes in
order to excite yourself to contrition for your
sins. During the first week of this month
review your general examination of conscience, and return to confession, accusing the
faults which God shall show you still in your
conscience. Every morning at the Communion of the Priest, recite the five acts before Communion, and then make a Spiritual
Communion, that is, excite in yourself a desire
of receiving sacramentally. I do not call this
a new practice, because it is contained in the
Holy Mass at which you have been assisting
daily since the first of May. Now, my dear

child, fly from the world as much as possible,
that you may be less exposed to offend God;
avoid all dangerous company ; observe, as much
as possible, solitude and silence ; be recollected,
and think only of that God so good and holy
whom you will soon receive FOR THE FIRST
TIME.

Following the example of St. Louis of
Gonzague, St. Stanislas Kostka, Blessed
Berchmans, Blessed Imelda, and many other
pious children, let the one thought of your
mind be your FIRST COMMUNION, the only
desire of your heart your FIRST COMMUNION
and the most frequent words on your lips, MY
FIRST COMMUNION MY FIRST COMMUNION.

RETREAT OF THREE DAYS BEFORE THE FIRST

COMMUNION.

The three days which precede your FIRST
COMMUNION should be consecrated to a retreat,
for in silence and recollection " Almighty God
will speak to your heart." If circumstances
prevent you from having a retreat in common,
ask your confessor to direct you in the exercises
of devotion to be used.

During retreat, my child, I will leave you entirely in the hands of your confessor, or him who preaches it ; follow the rules and advice given, and God will bless you. This retreat is made for two intentions :

1st. To excite you to repentance for your faults, and prepare you for your first general absolution.

2nd. To inflame you with a tender love for Jesus Christ, and dispose you the better to approach Him for the first time in the Sacrament of His love.

You should then assist at all the exercises of this retreat with these intentions, and return from each exercise with more repentance in your heart, and more love for our Divine Redeemer. Oh, my child, may the blessing of God descend upon you in this retreat, and procure you the unutterable consolation of a happy and holy Communion ?

IMPORTANT ADVICE.

I have still a few admonitions to give you, my child. The first is on the exercise of the ceremonies : take care that you do not act with levity. Although the host received is only bread yet it should be taken with respect and piety, because you will so soon receive the Body and Blood, Soul and Divinity of Jesus Christ. Children have often wept in the exercise of presenting themselves at the Table of the Lord. But a child who will amuse himself during these ceremonies will forget himself also on the day of his FIRST COMMUNION, or his recollection will be quite forced. With regard to the exterior preparation for your FIRST COMMUNION, I would recommend that you be not too much occupied with your dress, but think seriously of what it signifies before God.

The dress which is new, rich and beautiful, and which ornaments your body, is only a figure of the spiritual garments, that is, the virtues that should adorn your soul. This robe and veil so white for little girls, and the white badge which little boys wear on their left arm, signify the innocence and purity of their souls. The burning taper held in the hand signifies the flame of Divine Charity with which these young hearts should burn. I would advise you, after the ceremony, to have the taper blessed, and to keep it all your life, as a

souvenir of your FIRST COMMUNION. Place it
at the head of your bed, beside your crucifix, to
remind you of that great day ; and each year on
the anniversary of your FIRST COMMUNION light
it for a few minutes and mediatte what these
words signify: MY FIRST COMMUNION. Examine
yourself well —you will perhaps weep with
joy, or with repentance, according as you have
been faithful or ungrateful to God. The day
of your death this taper will brighten your
agony and serve as a symbol of faith to Jesus
when He comes to visit you for the last time
in the Holy Viaticum. The handsome prayer-
book which was given you by your dear
parents signifies the fervent supplication
which you should send up to the Throne of
Grace. Your friends and relations invited on
this joyful occasion represent the joy of the
angels and saints of Heaven, and that even
God Himself rejoices because you have received His Divine Son by a HOLY FIRST COM-
MUNION.

FIRST GENERAL ABSOLUTION.

It is on the eve of your FIRST COMMUNION
that you, my dear child, will receive for the

first time the General Absolution of all your
sins. It frequently happens that absolution
is given to children for sins confessed in early
childhood ; for would it not be sad if, having
committed a mortal sin at the dawn of reason,
you should have been all this time exposed
to the slavery of the devil and to eternal
damnation ? Far from us such a thought ! As
soon as a child is capable of sin, he should be
able also to receive the remedy of sin—*sacramental absolution.* St. Louis of Gonzague
at the age of eight or nine years received,
bathed in tears, *absolution* for two faults
which he had commited. The law of confessions obliges children to go to confession
when they have arrived at the age of reason,
that they may receive pardon for his sins,
for the confession without absolution does not
remit mortal sin. Certain precocious children
who think seriously of their salvation may
perhaps receive absolution many times before
their FIRST COMMUNION. On the General
Absolution, which you will receive, will
depend your good or your bad FIRST COM-
MUNION. Think seriously, my child, upon the
importance of this action, which may decide
your future happiness or misery.

Do not imitate those ignorant children who cast not even a thought on the General Absolution. Understand well the all-absorbing question which has occupied you so long, and which has penetrated you with a religious fear: Will my FIRST COMMUNION be good or bad ?

This important question will be decided at the moment you receive the first General Absolution. Prepare yourself then, dear child, with the greatest care to receive this absolution, and before going to receive it, ask yourself these two questions : 1st. Have I concealed or disguised any sin in my confession ? 2nd. Have I repented of all my faults, and taken the resolution never to offend God any more ? Do not go to receive absolution if your conscience does not respond *no* to the first question and *yes* to the second.

Pardon of Parents.

I *advise* you, my child, before receiving Absolution, to go and cast yourself at the feet of your father and mother, and ask pardon for all the faults committed against them. This practice, though not of obligation, and consequently a child will not sin by omitting it) is very agreeable to God, and will bring down special graces upon the child who performs it. You may ask pardon of your parents in whatever words your heart will dictate. After your parents have pardoned and kissed you, return again to your Father in heaven, and address Him in the following prayer:

Prayer of a child before going to receive General Absolution.

Having recited the prayers after the examination, page 57, and the ordinary prayer before each confession, page 76, continue:

My God, I firmly believe that Thou hast given Priests the power to remit sin. Alas! I have committed many sins since my baptism, but thou knowest, O God of goodness! that I have sincerely confessed them, and that in the bottom of my heart I bitterly repent of all my faults. With the assistance of Thy Holy grace I shall never more offend Thee. I go with confidence to Thee, in the person of my Confessor, to receive general absolution of all the faults of my childhood, hoping that it will efface them all from the book of judgment; purify me from all stain, restore to me in all its whiteness the robe of innocence; open to me the gates of Heaven, and close forever those of hell. Yes, oh! my God, I hope for all these miracles of mercy at the moment the Priest gives me absolution. If my dispositions are not sufficient, O my God! I conjure Thee, supply by Thy grace what is wanting in me.

Holy Angel Guardian, pray for me.

Holy Mary, pray for me, that I may receive a holy absolution.

After this prayer present yourself at the sacred Tribunal of Reconciliation, observing the advice and method of confession as in page 78.

Prayer after General Absolution.

Thou hast pardoned me, oh my God! and I am at length reconciled with Thee. Yes, all the sins of my childhood are effaced from the book of judgment; my soul has arisen from the grave of sin; the robe of innocence is restored to me as in my baptism; hell is closed, and heaven is open. How happy I would be to die now, and I do not wish to live longer unless to live and serve Thee. Grant me, O Lord, the grace to preserve until death the Divine friendship to which I have been restored by the sacramental absolution. Could I be so unfortunate as to offend again a God so good and merciful, a Father so tender? No, dear Lord. I would rather die a thousand times than to crucify Thee again by sin. Amen.

After this prayer continue your retreat, and do not leave it until to-morrow morning. Be careful not to commit the slightest fault, and sleep, my child, in the sweet and consoling thought of your FIRST COMMUNION, which you will receive to-morrow morning.

ESSENTIAL REMARKS.

First in washing your mouth to-morrow morning, out of respect for the Holy Communion, think of the great purity which should adorn your soul, and be careful not to swallow any drops of water.

Second—You know that in going to Communion you should be fasting, that is, you should not have taken either food or drink after midnight. It is through respect for the Adorable Body and Blood of Jesus Christ that the Church exacts this fast, which signifies that our souls must be as free from sin as our bodies are void of nourishment.

Take off your gloves before presenting yourself at the Holy Table. If the Sacred Host should stick to your mouth, you must not be disturbed, nor touch it with your fingers, but remove it with your tongue quietly and respectfully, then convey it down without allowing it to melt entirely in your mouth.

Good night! my dear child. Sleep in the happy peace of the Lord; sleep under the care of your good Angel, until the morning dawns of the bright and happy day.

> " Dream on, darling ! while thou'rt sleeping,
> Angels pure and bright
> Around thy cot their watch are keeping
> Through the silent night."

THE GREAT AND SOLEMN DAY, THE DAY OF MY FIRST COMMUNION.

Arise, child of benediction! the soft rays of the sun have already announced that the great day has arrived. Imagine that the Spouse of your soul calls you, in the words of the canticle, to joys unutterable: " Arise, make haste, my love, my dove, my beautiful one, and come. For winter is now past; the rain

is over and gone; the flowers have appeared
in our land; the time of pruning is come,—
the voice of the turtle is heard in our land.
The fig-tree hath put forth her green figs ; the
vines in flower yield their sweet smell. Arise,
my love, my beautiful one, and come."

The little birds have already begun their
sweet concerts, inviting you to sing the praises
of God. Come then, my child, come quickly.
Jesus calls you, He wishes to give Himself to
you for the first time. Is thy heart ready?
Prepare it still more, and sing the canticle of
joy, the celestial canticle the canticle of
divine love.

As for me, I shall assist in silence at the
touching spectcale, in union with the celestial
spirits. I have nothing to say to you, my
child, this morning, I am overpowered with
heavenly thoughts. Jesus will say all to you.

Remember, before going to the Temple of
God, to ask your parents' blessing, and having
received their heartfelt wishes, go to the arms
of Jesus, He waits for you, His heart is open
to receive you ; open your heart to Him who
wishes to give Himself to you for the first
time. Come, my child, the church is open, it

is decorated as on great feasts ; for, enter, you are the hero of this festival; take holy water, and to purify your soul from even its slightest stains, make upon your forehead the holy sign of the Cross.

There now, dearest child, I shall leave you with all confidence under the care of your holy pastor, who will direct and speak to you on this great and glorious day. In a retired spot of this holy temple I shall hear your sighs of love and gratitude, and behold your tears of the most tender devotion.

Farewell! dear child, may Mary direct your steps to the Altar of Jesus !

> " Sweet Jesus, may Thy Sacred Heart
> My hope and refuge be;
> There may I learn the heavenly art
> Of living but for Thee."

AFTERNOON

OF THE DAY OF THE FIRST COMMUNION.

Return of the Angel Guide to the First Communicant.

Angel.—Thy FIRST COMMUNION, dear child, is at length accomplished. Tell me, how dost thou feel now that thou possessest Jesus for the first time ? Wast thou really happy this morning, when the God of Heaven took up His abode in thy heart ?

Child.—Oh! yes, truly happy ; so much so, that I could not refrain my sighs and tears.

Angel.—Thy tears, my child, I witnessed, and thy tender sighs I heard; but thy heart, how did it feel, for I wish to rejoice with thee and bless the Lord ?

Child.—At that moment I was in raptures of happiness, my heart heaved with sighs, and from my eyes gushed fountains of tears. I was in heaven, or heaven was in my soul. Jesus, True God and True Man. His heart beating within His breast as it did when upon earth, His blood circulating in His veins, His eyes beaming on me, and His countenance radiant with love. I love Him with my whole heart. He speaks, and I listen; He speaks again and I weep, for His heavenly language overpowers me.

Angel.—Weep on, happy child, weep on, thy union with Jesus is consummated. His blood circulates in thy veins, and in an ecstasy of love thou canst exclaim—" I live now, not I, but Jesus liveth in me."

Child.—You have said it, I cannot. The

happiness I felt was celestial, O it was divine! I cannot think of it without tears.

Angel.—Thus in thy life there is one happy year, in this year there is one joyful month, in this month there is one celestial day, and in this day one moment of unutterable felicity.

Child.—O yes, the year, the month, the day, the moment of my FIRST COMMUNION!

Angel.—Engrave them, dear child, deeply in thy memoray and still more in thy heart. Tell me, canst thou understand how children could ever forget or cease to love the God of their FIRST COMMUNION?

Child.—No, for that I would require to have another heart than that which burned this morning with the flames of divine love. Snatch away from me this heart if you would have me cease to love Jesus; or if one sigh of mine should be the last for Him, may it be also the last of my life!

    " O Sacred Heart! sweet source from whence
       A stream of life e'er flows,
    The weary soul may draw from thence
       Refreshment and repose. "

Calm yourself, beloved child, forget for an instant the morning of this great day; the

evening also has its sweetness. The sun at
its setting still sends forth beautiful rays,
which may often be compared to a lovely
and bright aurora.

Two other ceremonies remain for this evening : the renewal of your Baptismal vows and
your consecration to the Most Blessed Virgin
Mother of God.

RENEWAL OF THE BAPTISMAL VOWS.

On the day of your baptism, my child, your
godfather and godmother renounced in your
name, the devil with all his works and pomps
and they promised that you would ever remain faithful to Jesus Christ, faithful to the
observance of His commandments and those
of His Church. Alas! since the age of reason,
how frequently have you perhaps sinned, and
become again the slave of the devil, following
his pomps, doing his works, and turning your
back on the Cross of Jesus? But you have
confessed and wept over your transgressions.
God has pardoned you, and now, my child, in
gratitude, consecrate yourself forever to Him
by renewing your baptismal vows. Go then,
my child, to the holy font, and standing be

fore the Crucifix, in presence of the holy Angels, with your right hand on the Missal, voluntarily and in a loud voice renew the solemn contract made by your godfather and godmother between you and God on the day of your baptism.

I believe firmly in God and in Jesus Christ, His only Son. I believe all the truths revealed in the Holy Gospel, and which the Catholic Church proposes to my belief.

I renew before God and His holy Angels all the engagements of my baptism.

I promise to observe, all my life, the commandments of God and of His holy Church. I renounce Satan, his pomps, and his works.

I unite myself with Jesus Christ forever.

CONSECRATION TO THE BLESSED VIRGIN.

From the Baptismal font, my child, go to the Altar of Mary, and 'prostrate at the feet of the Holy Virgin, Mother of God, consecrate yourself entirely to her, choosing her for your mother, declaring yourself her child, and putting yourself under her maternal protection till death.

ACT OF CONSECRATION.

Holy Virgin Mary, Mother of God, by virtue of the last words of Jesus on the Cross, " Behold thy Son, behold thy Mother, " I come and consecrate to you my childhood, my youth, and all my life. I choose you to-day for my mother, my advocate and my patron, and I declare myself your child. I wish to honor, to love, and to imitate you. I place under your holy protection the FIRST COMMUNION which I had the happiness to receive this morning; do not permit me, O blessed Mother, ever to abandon the God of goodness, who deigned this day to descend into my heart. Obtain for me the grace to remain faithful to Him unto death. It is done, Jesus is my heavenly brother. Mary, is my holy mother. Yes, I am a child of God, I shall also be a child of Mary. O holy Mother! deign to protect me during life, and especially at the hour of my death. Amen.

" Mary, sweetest Mother mine,
Make me be forever thine. "

⌐ After these two ceremonies, return,.my dear child, to your home, and take care not to aban-

don yourself to idle pleasure, but enter into a
holy joy and take some innocent recreation. Remember all your life that true joy
is found in piety and the possession of divine
love. Virtue is always gay because it is
always happy ; but never do or say anything
to afflict that God of love who has given Himself to you to-day in the Holy Communion.

, This evening, if the weather be fine, I would
advise you to take a little walk with your
parents or some of your companions of the
First Communion, but direct your steps to a
Calvary, or to some Church or Chapel dedicated to the Blessed Mother of God, and ere
the sun salutes you with his last rays, to
warn you that it is time for retiring, pay a
visit to the Blessed Sacrament, kneel also before the statue of the Blessed Virgin, and say
your rosary. When you shall have retired to
your room, piously say your night-prayer at
the foot of the Crucifix, examine your conscience, and sleep in the sweet thought, the
precious souvenir of your First Communion
which you received this morning.

DAY AFTER THE FIRST COMMUNION.

O what could my Jesus do more !
    And what greater blessing impart ?
O silence ! my soul, and adore
    And press Him still near to thy heart.

Mass of Thanksgiving.

Gratitude is a sacred duty : men exact it as their due ; with how much more reason should not God exact it ?

We must always thank the Lord for His blessings, and particularly for His great benefits. My child, what greater gift than the Holy Communion, return Him, then, your sincere gratitude. See now, my child, why the morning following the FIRST COMMUNION the children assemble again, and again assist at the Holy Sacrifice, which is called the Mass of Thanksgiving.

Do not forget my child, to assist piously ; the sight of the Altar, the baptismal font, and the altar of the Blessed Virgin, whence so many graces flowed into your soul, will bring forth anew your sighs and tears of gratitude. Try to feel over again the holy emotions which formed your happiness yesterday.

Make a spiritual communion at the Holy Mass, and recite again the acts after communion, which you will find in your prayer book.

SOUVENIR OF YOUR FIRST COMMUNION.

Man, on the achievement of any glorious victory, consecrates each year the anniversary to its memory; so with you, my child, the day of your FIRST COMMUNION is a day to be remembered throughout your whole life, and each year you should celebrate it religiously. This is the reason that the Pastor gives the first communicants a picture representing the august ceremony of the First Communion upon which is inscribed the name of the happy child, the year and month and day of this holy action, and the church in which it was performed. Preserve carefully this souvenir, which, with your taper, will warn you to celebrate piously every year the anniversary of that happy day of your FIRST COMMUNION.

DISTRIBUTION OF PRIZES.

To-day, probably, will be the general distribution of Catechism premiums. Will you receive any, my child? Perhaps you may, and perhaps you may not. This distribution should be for you the figure of the last judgment. What joy to receive a recompense! what regret to receive none! Judge then, my child, what will be your triumph at the last day, if you receive the eternal prize of Heaven, and what would be your despair if you should lose it. To-day if you do not receive a prize your only sorrow will be that you are not rewarded; but, at the last judgment, if you do not obtain the recompense of eternal felicity, your great sorrow will be accompanied with a second grief, that of seeing yourself not only deprived of an eternal recompense, but also consigned to eternal misery. Think seriously upon this, my child.

Nevertheless, I have a holy confidence in your piety, wisdom and diligence: these are the guarantees that you will receive premiums, and I congratulate you beforehand; only, take care not to yield to self-love. Preserve the souvenirs of your FIRST COMMUNION as happy foretokens of the celestial rewards which you may hope one day to receive for your piety and your wisdom.

MEMORANDUM OF EIGHT PAGES.

The day after your FIRST COMMUNION is also

a great day, and perhaps, my child, you do
not know how you should spend it, but I shall
tell you, and you will see how, simple as it is,
it will benefit you during your whole lifetime.
Make a little memorandum book of eight
pages and write,

On the first two pages, the principal sentiments of faith and piety which may have
affected you on the occasion of your First
Communion :

On the two following pages, your promises
and resolutions.

On the fifth and sixth, your rule of life.

On the last two write every year, on the
anniversary of your First Communion, a new
resolution and some good thought.

As an example, I will give you a copy of
one made by a pious youth in 1834, who continued to fill it up until 1841, the year of his
death.

MEMORANDUM BOOK OF EIGHT PAGES;

OR,

Resolutions and Holy Sentiments of the

FIRST COMMUNION.

1st.

GOOD SENTIMENTS.

Until the year of my FIRST COMMUNION I was very giddy and very thoughtless; alas! I have often offended God and caused sadness to my dear parents. But, the first day of the year, my dear mother, after wishing me a happy New Year and the grace to make a good FIRST COMMUNION, put into my hands a book entitled The Angel Guide; or, Year of the FIRST COMMUNION. At that instant I felt myself quite changed, and, kissing her tenderly, I said : console yourself, dear mamma, you will yet be happy, I promise you.

God gave me grace to keep my word.

Accordingly, as I approached the time of making my FIRST COMMUNION, I felt more faith and piety within my soul.

I regretted more and more having offended God in the first and most acceptable years of life, often saying with St. Augustine : " Too late have I known Thee : too late have I loved Thee ! "

I have often been saddened at the sight of a crucifix, and have sometimes bathed in tears the wounds of my crucified Saviour.

The 25th March, Feast of the Blessed Virgin, I besought her with all my heart to obtain for me the grace to receive worthily my FIRST COMMUNION, and I remained a long time at her feet, without being able to restrain my tears. Still, I felt very happy, for it appeared to me she said from time to time : Stay, my child, with me a little longer, for I love you dearly. "

On Good Friday, the contemplation of our dear Lord's sufferings afflicted me much, and gave me a lively sorrow for the sins which caused His sufferings and death.

2nd Page.—CONTINUATION OF GOOD DISPOSITIONS.

When, in the beginning of May, I was examined for my FIRST COMMUNION, I wept at the same time with joy, and with sorrow, saying to myself: I shall never more offend God. I shall love Him now and forever.

Ten days before my FIRST COMMUNION, my general confession being finished, my confessor having told me that I was received, I could not contain myself with joy. My God! I exclaimed, how good and merciful art Thou to a child so miserable and unworthy as I am!

I began my retreat with varied feelings of joy and sadness, hope and fear.

The sermon which touched my heart most was the one on the Prodigal Son. I, too, said with all my heart, "*My God! I have sinned against Heaven and before Thee, and I am not worthy to be called Thy child.*" I represented myself at the Holy Table, sitting at the side of Jesus Christ, like the Prodigal beside his father.

The act of contrition on the last day of the retreat almost broke my heart.

In receiving the general absolution of all my sins, I felt myself relieved as from an enormous weight.

I did not sleep much the eve of my FIRST COMMUNION. I could not, and during the little time I slept I dreamed of the Holy Table and my FIRST COMMUNION.

The day of my FIRST COMMUNION, I felt that it was the happiest day of my life, and I shall never forget it.

The consecration to the Blessed Virgin made me very happy.

This morning again, I felt very much affected on thinking of the happiness of yesterday, and I asked myself: Edward, will you ever be so ungrateful as to abandon the God of your FIRST COMMUNION? Do you not see that, since you have begun to be wise and love Almighty God, that you are much happier, and that thus you render your dear Parents happier also? Come, Edward, give yourself wholly to God forever. O dearest Lord, let me be Thine forever, and thou, O Mary! receive me also as thy child, for how can I love Jesus without loving thee, the most tender and affectionate of Mothers?

During my retreat I compared God with the world and the world with God, and I said to myself, God, my first Master, my first Father, and my first King, is infinitely more than the world, or rather the world is nothing when compared with God. I take, then, the resolution to fear God more than the world, never to be ashamed of my religious duties before men, and to despise their judgments when there is question of serving the Lord.

The day of my FIRST COMMUNION, I compared my body with my soul and my soul with my body, and I became satisfied that my soul, living and immortal image of the Divinity, is infinitely more precious than my body, and I promised Almighty God that for the rest of my life I would occupy myself a great deal more with my soul than with my body.

This morning in thanking God for my happiness in being united with Him in the Holy Communion, I thought of heaven, and I said to myself, how insignificant is earth when compared to heaven! I took the resolution to sacrifice this world, and everything here below, to merit heaven. I compared this life with eternity, and I said, What folly, for sixty or seventy years, at the most, to risk an eternity of happiness! No, on the contrary, I take the resolution to employ the present life entirely in meriting for myself a happy and blissful eternity.

The sins of my childhood afflicted me much at the time of my FIRST COMMUNION. Shall I sin again and prepare new griefs for myself, and add to the sufferings of my Beloved Saviour? No, dear Lord, I promise you never to sin again.

I have been so happy since I entered upon the path of virtue, and would I leave it now? Oh, no, I shall never leave it. How miserable was I, when following the ways of sin, but I shall never return to them. I desire, by my good conduct, to console my dear parents whom I so often afflicted before my FIRST COMMUNION. I shall obey them in all things.

I shall attend the Catechism of Perseverance as much as possible.

4th Page.—CONTINUATION OF RESOLUTIONS.

I shall keep only good company, and I hope never again to commit a mortal sin. No, my God, never; but, if I should ever be so unhappy as to fall, I promise Thee not to sleep one night in enmity with Thee; I shall go to confession that very day, lest death should overtake me.

I wish to wear continually some objects of piety, particularly a crucifix and a medal of the Blessed Virgin, that, should I die suddenly, I may be at once recognized as a Catholic.

I purpose to make a little oratory in my bedroom with pious pictures, a crucifix, and statue of the Blessed Virgin, also a holy water font, and here I shall say my prayers night and morning.

I shall cultivate a particular devotion to my holy guardian angel, recommending myself to him every morning, and every night, and from time to time during the course of the day.

I shall not forget to honor equally St. Edward, my patron Saint.

I shall not read any doubtful books, without asking my Confessor whether it would be sinful or not.

I shall consult my parents in all things, and follow their wise admonitions.

I shall follow the advice given us by our Catechist, and read attentively a chapter of the Catechism every Sunday, and every Festival, also that which explains the mystery of the day.

The preacher of the retreat told us when any child of our neighborhood woud die to visit the mortal remains in order to make more serious reflections on the uncertainty of life.

I desire to form my character to civility, meekness and kindness, in which virtues are constituted the happiness of society and of the family.

I shall try to have a heart that compassionates the poor, the sick, and the afflicted. I shall relieve them if I can; at least, I will try to comfort them.

5th Page.—MY RULE OF LIFE.

Made the day after my First Communion, June 16th, 1834.

In the name of the Father, and of the Son, and of the Holy Ghost, Amen. I desire, O Lord! to be truly Thine, and to lead a life more and more agreeable to Thee, and for this reason, in the presence of all the Saints and Angels of heaven, especially of my holy Angel Guardian, I take the following resoultions, to which I hope to be faithful unto death, through Thy holy grace and the protection of the Blessed Virgin:

Every Day.

1st. I shall observe faithfully the commandments of God and His Church, and the duties of my state of life.

2nd. I shall rise and retire to rest, as much as possible, at regular hours.

3rd. I shall, on awaking, give my first thoughts to God, my first words being Jesus and Mary, and my first action the sign of the cross. At night, I shall sanctify my repose in a similar manner.

4. I shall be faithful to say my prayers every morning, humbly kneeling at the foot of my crucifix.

5th. I shall begin my principal action by a short prayer or elevation of my soul to God.

6th. I shall think often of God during the day.

7th. I shall try to say, every day, at least a decade of my Rosary.

8th. Every night I shall make an examination of conscience.

Every Week.

9th. On Sunday I shall try and give some alms to the poor for the love of God.

10th. Every Thursday, as much as possible, I shall hear Mass.

6th Page.—RULE OF LIFE CONTINUED.

11th. On Friday I shall practise some act of mortification at meals, or say five *Paters* or five *Aves]* in honor of the Passion of our Lord.

12th. On Saturday I shall say the third part of the Rosary, in honor of the Blessed Virgin.

Every Month.

13th. I shall go to confession every month, and shall strive to render myself worthy to approach Holy Communion.

14th. I shall apply myself to correct one of my defects.

Every Year.

15th. I shall celebrate religiously, every year, the anniversary of my Baptism, of my FIRST COMMUNION, and of my Confirmation.

Of my Baptism, 27th March.

Of my FIRST COMMUNION, 15th June.

Of my Confirmation, 22nd July.

16th. I shall endeavor to make each year a little retreat of two or three days.

17th. The last day of each month I shall read over this rule of life, by way of examination. I shall also read the good sentiments and resolutions, and shall impose upon myself a punishment for any infidelities of which I shall find myself guilty, terminating by this prayer:

Pardon me, Oh ! my God, the faults which 1 have committed against this rule and these resolutions of my FIRST COMMUNION, and particularly those which I have committed against your commandments and those of Your Holy Church, during the month which has just passed. Grant me the grace to observe them with more exactitude during the month which is about to begin. I ask this grace through the merits of Your Divine Son and the intercession of Mary His Holy Mother, Amen,

July 1st.

I am here again, Father, you see how faithful I am to come.

Very well, my child, and how are we with the God of our FIRST COMMUNION?

Well, Father.

Have you been faithful?

Yes, Father.

God be praised, my child! think what you must be for the edification of the family, and even of the parish. You must lead a truly pious and fervent life, and take care that you do not relax from the fervor of your FIRST COMMUNION.

Oh, no, Father.

Examine if you have not, without perceiving it, relapsed into one or other of your bad habits.

Oh, no, Father, I have wept too much over them to begin again.

Have you read your little memorandum the last day of the month?

Yes, Father.

And have you been faithful to all?

Yes, Father, except that I was once lazy in getting up in the morning, and that I had not time to say my prayers.

Oh! take care, my child, it is thus that one begins, and by little and little one may go a great distance.

But, oh! Father, I repented of it in my examination of conscience that night, and I have promised never to do so again.

That is well, my child.

To-morrow will be a Feast of the Blessed Virgin, recommend yourself to her powerful protection.

Now, my child, some of these first days of the month, go to confession. I advise you, for the future, to go every month.

Yes, Father, I promise, for I wish always to love that God of mercy who has deigned to give Himself to me in the Holy Communion.

"What happiness can equal mine?
I've found the object of my love;
My Jesus dear, my King Divine,
Has come to me from Heaven above,"

CONFIRMATION.

Come, Holy Ghost! I humbly pray!
Shed on my mind a cheering ray
 Of Thine effulgence bright.
Come Thou, the Father of poor!
Of every gift the kind Bestower,
 The heart's enlivening light!

Probably during this month, my child, you will have the happiness of receiving the fourth Sacrament, that of Confirmation; at all events it is well to receive it as soon as possible. Take care not to imitate certain children who neglect to receive this great Sacrament. They give reason to fear that they did not bring to their FIRST COMMUNION a sufficient preparation; or, at least, that they have been unfaithful to that great grace.

As to you, my child, be faithful to receive it with the proper dispositions. Make a retreat of a day or two, and, during that time of grace, review your conscience since your general confession. On the day of Confirmation, renew your fervor, and revive the holy sentiments of your FIRST COMMUNION. Employ the rest of the month in thanksgiving for this new grace, thinking often of the Holy Ghost whom you have received, asking more and more His seven gifts, and be faithful to correspond to them. In reciting the Creed for the future say with lively faith, I believe in the Holy Ghost, and on the anniversary of your Confirmation, try each year to receive Holy Communion, and thus strengthen your love for that Holy Spirit.

AUGUST 1ST.

I have come to see you, this evening, f or it has been announced in the pulpit to-day that we would make our Second Communion on the 15th of this month, the Feast of the glorious Assumption of the Blessed Virgin, and I have come to ask you for any advice you may deem necessary.

Well, my child, I would advise you to approach the Holy Communion every year on that day: one Communion in the year to honor the Blessed Virgin is not too much.

No, Father, two Communions would not be too much, I think.

Certainly not, but begin by one; and as the Assumption is one of the most beautiful of our Dear Mother's Feasts, it will be well to give it the preference and communicate on that great day. In all your Communions, my child, do not forget the example of St. Louis of Gonzaga, who always made three days preparation, and three days of thanksgiving. The eve of this feast is a fast: as you are not of the age to fast, viz., twenty-one years, you are only obliged to abstain; you may take a little less breakfast or practise some other mortification, such as depriving yourself of sweetmeats, confectionery, &c.

Before leaving, my child, I would like to question you a little.

Father, it pleases me much to know that you are still my Angel Guide.

Well, my child, have you always been faithful to give your heart to God in the morning, and to close your eyes in sleep by recommending yourself to the Divine protection ?

Yes, Father, I have never forgotten, except five or six times since my FIRST COMMUNION. and besides mamma has placed a holy water font at the head of my bed, and recommended me to take some holy water night and morning, and to make the sign of the cross.

It is an excellent practice, my child.

I think, Father, I sleep more tranquilly when I do it.

You have a dear good mother, my child, and you should love her much, and thank God for giving her to you.

Tell me again, my child, have you not omitted, through negligence or human respect, the excellent practice of saying grace before and after meals ?

No, Father. I did sometimes forget it, but it was not through negligence, and still less through human respect.

Very well, my child, I am perfectly satisfied with you ; come and see me every month until the end of the year.

Yes, Father, twice a month, if you will permit me.

No, once is sufficient, but attend faithfully to your examination of conscience. Adieu, my child, pray for me, and I shall pray for you.

> " Blessed Virgin, think of me,
> Sailing on this stormy sea ;
> Lead me onward through the strife,
> Guide me safe to endless life. "

1st September.

LET us begin, my child, by the examina_ tion of your conscience. Have you said your morning and evening prayers, or do you content yourself, now, with those little prayers said in childhood, or which *ignorant* or *lazy* people make use of ?

Well, Father, seven or eight times that I

was sleepy at night, and twice or three times that I was lazy in the morning, I did not say my long prayers.

Ah, my child, that was, wrong; you must return to your first fervor and exactitude, without which all will be lost. But tell me, those nights, you did not make your examination of conscience either ?

No, Father, I did not, but I promise you that I will from this day forth.

Well, my child, general pardon for the past, in the hopes of a better future. Listen to me now attentively.

CATECHISM OF PERSEVERANCE.

Catechism will begin this month if it has not already begun. Go faithfully, my child, to the Catechism of Perseverance, without this I fear you will not persevere in virtue. Make a practise of reading attentively, every Sunday a lesson or two out of your Catechism, and every Holy-day the lesson of the Feast itself. This will enable you to pass over the whole of your Catechism during the year, so as never to forget it, but especially to reduce it to practice.

Yes, Father, I shall do so.

I advise you, my dear child, to make your Third Communion on the 8th of September, the Feast of the Nativity of the Blessed Virgin, if your Confessor shall permit. Without doubt you will every year of your life celebrate the birthday of your Heavenly Mother, a day which should make you very happy. Love, my child, this immaculate Mother ; and she will take you by the hand in the journey of life, and at the hour of death will throw her mantle over you, that no harm may befall you. I advise you, if your Confessor approve of it, to be enrolled in the confraternity of the Holy Scapular. Remember, always, that in practices of piety, as well as of penance, we should do nothing without consulting the guide of our conscience.

COMMUNION MORE OR LESS FREQUENT.

Tell me, Father, how often should I go to Communion each year ? I put in my little memorandum every month, or at least on all great Festivals. Is that too little or too much ?

It is not, my child, for me to decide. Communion, more or less frequent, depends on the virtues or defects, spiritual needs, family or social position, &c., of each one.

It is only the Confessor who can decide that. I refer you then to yours, my child, on this question, contenting myself with saying, in general, that the two rules the most adopted and, according to all appearances, the wisest in this respect, are, *every month* for children who can easily do so, who feel an attraction, and whom their Confessor judges worthy: *every three months*, for children who are in the employ of others, or who do not feel the desire to communicate more frequently, and to whom their Confessor does not advise it. There might be made a third class of children, between the two preceding, and whom I would advise to receive on the seven or eight principal Feasts of the year. You see, my child, that these confessions and communions more or less frequent, are only of devotion. Strictly speaking, your duty is expressed in the two Commandments given below:

" To confess your sins at least once a year,

" To receive worthily the Blessed Eucharist at Easter or within the time appointed."

The least that you can do every year for the future, is, to confess and receive the Holy Communion at Easter, or within the Pascal time. For anything beyond this, I refer you to your Confessor.

Come again, my child, on the first of October, for I have many things, some of importance, to say to you.

Oh! tell me now, Father, please.

No, my child, I have said enough for to-day. I see you are a little curious and impatient, and you must accustom yourself to mortify this haste to know at once what it is not necessary for you to know yet.

It is true, Father, and I shall profit by this admonition. Please give me your blessing before I go.

OCTOBER 1ST.

HERE I am again, dear Father, quite disposed to hear your important advice, and to try and reduce it to practice.

Before giving it, my child I have a few questions to ask: Have you been enrolled in the Scapular?

Yes, Father.

And do you say every day the seven *Paters* and seven *Aves* enjoined?

Yes, Father, I forgot them only twice. Was that a sin, Father

No, my child, these prayers are not of obligation, they are merely devotional, and, even if they were of obligation, when the forgetfulness is quite involuntary, there is no sin.

Tell me, my child, what did your Confessor remark as to the number of times you should approach the Holy Communion during the year?

Seven or eight times, Father, that is on the principal Feasts; he does not think me as yet strong enough in piety and virtue to receive every month.

You see, my child, you are of the intermediate class of which I spoke the last time; without knowing altogether your conscience, it is about the same judgment I formed of you.

Ah! you know it pretty well, Father.

Now, my child, I wish to examine you upon your conduct during this month. Do you still go regularly to Mass and Vespers on Sunday, or do you work on that day?

Oh, no, I do not work at all, and Mamma would not allow me either, but I missed Vespers once, much against my will, but Mamma, who is so pious, said I would not sin.

How did you spend the afternoon?

I said my Vespers with Mamma, and then we went to the Church in the evening and made a visit to the Blessed Sacrament, and said the Rosary.

That is well, my child. During this month another Feast of the Blessed Virgin occurs, Rosary Sunday. May she who was saluted by Gabriel as Mother of God prove a powerful protectress and a loving Mother to you.

> Hail Mary, full of grace! with thee
> The Lord vouchsafes to dwell:
> In greeting strain did Gabriel thus
> His heavenly message tell.

CHOICE OF A STATE OF LIFE.

Listen, my child, to this important advice.

Some time after the FIRST COMMUNION, the generality of young persons choose a state of life; perhaps, my child, that during this month you also will choose yours, that is to say that you will tear yourself away from the tender embraces of your parents, and quit the home of your childhood, to begin a career which you will follow until death. Listen attentively, I pray you.

Yes, Father.

Weigh well the great truth which I tell you?

Yes, Father.

Salvation or damnation depends, very generally, *upon the choice of a state of life.*

Is it true, Father?

Yes, my child. God, in the designs of His Providence, creating man to perpetuate society, calls each one to a particular state of life, and it is to this particular state, and no other, that He attaches the special graces for his salvation. If he embraces that state to which God calls him, and to which are attached the special graces of his salvation, he will easily save his soul, his salvation is even ensured, provided that he corresponds faithfully to grace; but, if he embrace any other state to which God does not call him, and to which, consequently, the special graces of salvation are not attached for him, he will be saved with great difficulty, and even his salvation is in great danger, because he will find in that state a multitude of obstacles, and he will not find the particular graces to triumph over them?

Do you understand, my child?

Yes, Father.

E

It is necessary, at this decisive epoch, to know and embrace the state to which Almighty God calls you.

But how shall I know the way in which I should walk?

THE MEANS OF KNOWING THE STATE OF LIFE TO WHICH GOD CALLS YOU.

1st. Above all, think seriously of the salvation of your immortal soul, of God, Heaven and Eternity; say to yourself, like young Edward, in his memorandum of eight pages: God is greater than the world; my soul is greater than my body; heaven is greater than earth; eternity is greater than time. In the choice of a state of life, I must consult more the interests of God, of my soul of heaven, of eternity, than those of the world, the body, earth and time; for what will it avail me to be rich and honoured upon earth, happy, according to the world, if I lose my soul for all eternity? These first considerations will dispose you to make a wise and prudent choice.

2nd. Before going further, desire seriously to know the state to which God calls you, and be resolved to embrace it.

3rd. When you have these happy dispositions fully established, pray fervently that God may enlighten you, that you may not be deceived in so important a choice.

4th. Consult death, my child, *his judgment*, says the Holy Ghost, *is wise and good*; that is to say, place yourself in spirit on the bed of death, and ask yourself: " *When I shall be on the point of death, and about to appear before God, what state would I wish to have embraced in my youth and lived all my life?* " And do not enter any state which you would regret to have entered at the hour of death.

5th. Consult your parents, since, above all, they are religious and before God occupy themselves with your eternal salvation much more than your worldly happiness. Yes, consult your parents; it is the duty of a child: and it is in the designs of God that fathars and mothers should direct their children in so important a choice.

6th. Give some little alms for that intention.

7th. Consult, principally, your Confesscr, after having made yourself well known to him.

He is on this point the principal organ of the Holy Spirit in regard to you.

8th. In fine, when you are about definitely to fix your choice, recite the *Veni Creator*, or Come Holy Ghost, for nine days, to implore the light of that Divine Spirit. If you seek in all simplicity of heart the will of God He will direct you by means of those whom He has placed over you, and, in following their decision, you will embrace the state to which He calls you. If, in spite of all these precautions you should be mistaken and embrace another state than that to which God called you, He would bless you even in your error, by reason of the purity of your intention, and, rather than suffer you to perish, He would transfer to you the graces of sanctification which He had intended for you in that other state.

Do not forget that the last day of the month is a day of fasting and abstinence; be careful not to eat meat on that day, and practise some little acts of mortification. Read on that day your little memorandum of FIRST COMMUNION. Go, my child, and may God bless you!

NOVEMBER 1st.

To drink of Life's eternal spring
My thirsty soul desires,
And longs to find that holy stream,
To quench its parching fires.

GOOD afternoon, my child; all in smiles ?
your countenance bespeaks joy, you seem
to be very happy ?

O yes, dear Father, I had the happiness
of going to Holy Communion this morning,
and my Confessor has permitted me to go
again to-morrow ; two communions in succes-
sion ! my soul is filled with happiness.

I fully understand, my child, the happiness
of which you speak : to-day you went to Holy
Communion to honor all the saints of God,
and to ask their prayers, that you, too, may be
one of their number ; to-morrow you will
communicate for the souls in Purgatory. Make
special mention of deceased friends (among
whom you will not forget him to whose
memory this little work is dedicated). God
grant he may not need your prayers ! but,
though in Heaven, he will lovingly think of
his children of earth, and ask for them many
blessings. Remember, also, in your charity,

those who have labored for your sanctification, your Pastors and teachers, and also her who has translated this little work for your instruction. (Perhaps, ere you read these lines, she, too, may have passed into eternity.) My child, never forget this pious practise of going to Holy Communion every year of your life for the suffering souls in Purgatory. Alas! those friends whom we loved so dearly may be burning in those devouring flames, weeping and sighing for the day of their deliverance.

What a happiness if by our prayers and communions we release them from their sufferings and open Heaven to them! Therefore, during your whole life, be very particular in praying for the dead, but, above all, for your parents when they die. Many children have the pious custom of saying one *Pater* and one *Ave* every day, at their morning prayer, for their relations who are living, and again at their evening prayer for their relations who are dead. My child, this is an excellent custom, what do you think of adopting it?

I shall begin, Father, this very night.

Let us return now to the examination of conscience; since your FIRST COMMUNION do you not sometimes eat meat on Friday or days of abstinence ?

Oh! Father, that is too much, you know very well I do not. I would rather die.

Alas ! my child, this world is very bad, and you need not be surprised if the most sacred duties of religion are held up to ridicule, and if your abstinence should be laughed at !

Well, no matter, they may laugh as much as they like, and if all in the world should eat meat, I shall not eat it.

Take care, my child, to say that would be presumption. It was thus that St. Peter protested to our Lord that he would remain faithful to Him, and the same night he denied Him.

It is true, but I love God too much, Father, to offend Him thus.

There it is again, my child, your presumption makes me tremble for you; God almost always punishes the presumptuous by a deplorable fall from grace.

Come again on the first of December. Meantime I shall pray for your happy persever. ance.

November 23rd.

"There is a home for weary souls,
  By sin and sorrow driven ;
When toss'd on life's tempestuous shoals,
Where storms arise, and ocean rolls,
  And all is drear, but heaven ! "

SORROWFUL RETURN OF THE CHILD

Ah ! it is you again, my child. What is wrong with you, and why are you so sad ?

Father, I have come before the day ap. pointed. I met with a great misfortune. You know that yesterday was Friday?

Very well, there was no harm in that.

But, Father, I was at dinner at one of my friends who was not a good Catholic, and the family all eat meat. I would not at first take it, but they made such fun of me that I got ashamed, and I took some and eat it. Alas ! Father, I committed a mortal sin, did I not ?

Without answering that sorrowful question, my child, I wish to remark all the turns of your little self-love. Now, listen to what I say : it was not necessary for you to tell me that *yesterday was Friday—that you were at dinner at a friend's house—that these friends were not good Catholics—that they all ate meat*—that is our own business, and not yours—*that you did not want to eat it.* First excuse to diminish your sin, *but they made such fun of you.* Second excuse, that *you felt ashamed.* Third excuse, and *that you took it and ate it.* Ah! at last you have fully arrived at the sin. I HAVE EATEN MEAT ON A DAY FORBIDDEN. This is all you should have said, and not taken the roundabout way in which you expressed yourself. Such is the manner in which the Confessor's time is so frequently taken up with useless questions, excuses and explanations, all to satisfy self-love. Say simply, Father, I have done so and so, nothing more, unless a circumstance would increase the sin. Now, my child, to answer your question, you have committed a grievous transgression. What was it I told you the last time, when you thought you were stronger then Peter ? Was it not that God would punish your presumption ? Learn, then, my child to distrust yourself, and in all your promises and resolutions always to add, *with the grace of God.* Without His grace we are nothing, and we can do nothing. However, do not be discouraged, God is merciful, He will pardon you; do not remain in this state, but go quickly to Confession, lest you might die, and never enter His heavenly Kingdom.

Oh! Father, I have already been to Confession. I could not bear it any longer, I was so unhappy. I cried almost the whole day, and in the evening I went to Confession, and my Confessor treated me very kindly. I feared he would scold me, and not allow me to go to Holy Communion at Midnight Mass at Christmas. He said I did well to come immediately to Confession, and that he would give me absolution, but to return on Saturday, that I might go to holy Communion on the first Sunday of Advent. Father, after so great a sin, should I go to Communion on Sunday?

My child, obey in all things your Confessor: allow him to be your guide, and do not pretend to guide yourself. God inspired you with the thought of going to Confession immediately, which if you did not do you would perhaps continue in sin, lay aside your exercises of piety, and finally lose your soul. The reason that so many young persons do not persevere is that they become discouraged at their first fall, and neglect Confession; then the devil seduces them into new sins which soon become habitual, and they lose their souls. If like you, they went to Confession after their first sin, their Confessor would absolve them, and after a few days would have them go to Communion. They would receive in that absolution, and especially in that Communion, new strength to turn from their evil ways and resist the devil.

Profit, then, my child, of your own experience, and if it should happen you, which God forbid! to sin against any commandment whatsoever, go and confess the same day if possible, and try to go very soon to Communion. This is the way to diminish the number of your faults, and to correct them entirely. All Confessors will advise it, for it is the sovereign remedy against your passions.

Father, I may communicate in peace on Sunday?

Certainly, my child.

Thanks, Father, I feel much happier. I shall come all the same on the 1st of December.

Yes, yes; go now, my child, for I am rather in a hurry.

Farewell, Father.

December 1st.

The Winter's cold and Summer's heat,
In Heaven is not known;
Sweet flowers *there* forever bloom,
For Springtime n'er has flown.

BEHOLD! my child, the last month of the year of your FIRST COMMUNION has arrived. Oh! how quickly has this most beautiful year of your life passed away! a year never to be forgotten. It remains for you to sanctify the few remaining days ere they, too, be engulfed into eternity. The holy season of Advent, which we begin this month, is, in the spirit of the Church, a time of expiation, of sighs, of tears, and of prayers, and, at the same time, one of desires, of piety and fervor, to prepare us for the coming of Jesus Christ. Do not forget it, my child, through the course your life.

During this month I have three instructions of the highest importance to give you—the first on the crises and storms of youth, an age which you must soon traverse; the second, on the manner of combating your passions; the third on perseverance. But for to-day we will limit ourselves to the first.

Heretofore, my child, you have had only
the lesser combats to sustain against the world,
the devil and your own heart, in order to ensure the triumph of virtue within you, and to
prove yourself faithful to the God of your
childhood and of your FIRST COMMUNION, and
notwithstanding, you have already told me
several times how painful were these combats. Well, my child, be it known to you
that the whole life of man is a warfare of this
kind, and until a certain age this combat
for you will be on the increase, but especially during youth it will be most terrible.
Yes, in a few years more, my child, passions
the most violent, which, perhaps as yet you
do not even know, will arise in your heart;
the devil, will redouble his efforts to destroy
you, and the world, by a multitude of snares,
artifices, scandals, and occasions of sin, will
declare against you a relentless war, to with-
draw you from virtue, and lead you into vice.

Oh! Father, how you frighten me!

I do so designedly, that, being warned of the
danger, you may be less surprised at its

approach, and that, fearing it beforehand, you may be stronger to resist.

But what must I do, Father, to hold out in this triple war against the world, the devil, and my own heart?

In the first place, my child, you must have recourse to the spiritual arms of which the Apostle St. Paul speaks; you are still young, but already a soldier of Jesus Christ by Confirmation; take His complete armor, which is composed of *a coat of mail, a shield, a helmet, a girdle and a sword.*

But, Father, what does all that mean? This war of which you speak is truly terrible.

Yes, my child, and without this armor, you cannot be victorious. Listen to the explanation of this spiritual armor which St. Paul himself gives: " Put you on the armor of God, that you may be able to stand against the deceits of the devil. Stand, therefore, having your loins girt about with truth, and having on the breastplate of justice; and your feet shod with the preparation of the Gospel of peace, in all things taking the shield of faith, wherewith you may be able to distinguish all the fiery darts of the wicked one. And take unto you the helmet of salvation, and the word of the spirit (which is the word of God)." When you are enveloped with the armor of the Lord, count it still as nothing if you do not add the most important of all, which is prayer. " Watch and pray that you enter not into temptation." Thus, my child, during the boisterous age of youth, when the world, the devil, and your own passions are so violent, in order to obtain the victory, it is necessary that faith, confidence in God, meditation on His Divine word, and fervent prayer, should everywhere accompany you.

1st. *Faith.*—Let your memory come back incessantly to the great truths of faith which you now believe,—the existence of God, your Creator and first Master, the spirituality and immortality of your soul, Heaven, Hell, Eternity. Strengthen your belief more and more in these truths, the thought of which will make it difficult for you to sin.

2nd. *Confidence in God.*—Be fully persuaded that, if of yourself you can do nothing, with grace you can do all things. This grace you can always obtain by asking it.

3rd. *Meditation on the Word of God.*—The

Word of God must be heard, read often, medi-tated, digested, as it were, by serious reflections, in order to penetrate your soul with the fear of His judgments and the hope of His rewards

4th. *Prayer.*—Pray at the moment of temptation, calling on the Lord to assist you, and at all times by a constant fidelity to your exercises of piety.

Without this spiritual armor, my child, these violent tempests with which youth is beset would force you from the path of virtue and divine love, and plunge you into the abyss of sin and the slavery of the devil. But with these arms of God's grace you will repel the suggestions of the demon of impurity, and you will preserve the happy liberty of the children of God which you now enjoy. Go, my child, and meditate upon what I have told you, but, before going, tell me, have you been faithful to the Catechism of Perseverance?

Yes, Father, and I hope to go for a long time yet.

Return on the 12th of the month, and I shall continue my instructions on the manner in which you must combat your passions.

December 12th.

Spiritual Combat.

FATHER, already I have had need of the spiritual arms of which you spoke in your last instruction. I really believe that this war of youth has begun for me ; in many places where I have gone people have laughed at me because I tried to be faithful to my religious duties, and they even sought to lead me into evil. The devil put into my mind a crowd of bad thoughts, and my heart itself, somewhat shaken, seemed also to carry me away. But, Father, I had recourse immediately to the shield of faith, the helmet of salvation, and the sword of the Spirit; with these, together with the anchor of hope, and the all-powerful arms of prayer, you so often recommended, I continued faithful to God. And that God of bounty has recompensed me, for I have tasted the greatest consolations in my prayers and exercises of piety.

Yes, my child, you are right, that is the beginning of the warfare of youth of which I have spoken to you. You can always, as you have just done, carry the victory against those three sworn enemies of your salvation—the devil, the world, and your own heart. Know, that almost always after the victory you will taste those ineffable consolations which God afterwards gave you. This, my child, is the happiness of virtue, which we call spiritual joy, divine unction, foretaste of Heaven, and which sustains the true Christian in the battles of the Lord; whereas, if you had yielded to evil you would have been immediately punished by the remorse which would prey upon your heart, and the terrible vacuum into which it would fall. You made the experience of it the last month.

Oh! it is so true, Father; what a difference!

Now, since you profit so well by the advice which I give you, I shall instruct you upon the manner of combating your passions, which I shall reduce to five principal means; meditation prayer, counsel, combat, examination.

1st. *Meditation*—Whatever be the passion which tyrannizes over you, and which you wish to overcome, but especially if it be any impure passion, say to yourself: " *I have always been miserable when I allowed myself to be drawn away by this passion, and I shall be always miserable as long as I remain a slave to it. On the contrary, I have always been happy when I triumphed over it, and I shall be always happy when I shall have overcome it again. If I am damned, it will be in consequence of this passion, and I shall not be saved if I do not gain a victory over it. If I only wish I will be able to triumph over it : for God will not permit me to be tempted beyond my strength. He always gives sufficient grace for salvation. I know by experience that the victory is mine, if I choose to resist."*

The previous reflections, which we call meditation, are necessary for you to convince yourself of the necessity of the combat, and the victory, and also to determine thereto your own will.

2nd. *Prayer*—Prayer supposes diffidence in ourselves, and confidence in God; direct towards this passion, in order to destroy it, all your exercises of piety : Meditation, Mass, Rosary, and Visits to the Blessed Sacrament; that is, offer them to God for this intention, and say particular prayers for the same end, invoking the intercession of the Blessed Virgin, your Angel Guardian and holy patrons, &c.

3rd. *Counsel.*—Open your heart in regard to this unhappy passion, which predominates in you, to a wise and enlightened Director, conceal nothing from him, and, after having consulted him, obey him in all things, thus, you will be victorious.

4th. *Combat.*—Make vigorous attacks upon this passion, refusing without pity all its cravings, and doing, on the contrary, everything to mortify it.

5th. *Examination.*—In the general examination of your conscience, which you make every night, and which I cannot too much recommend to you, look closely to this passion, and bring yourself to an exact account of the victories you will have gained, or defeats, alas! which you will have sustained.

Be sure, my child, if you are faithful to employ these five means, sooner or later, and even very soon, you will carry a complete victory, and your happiness and glory in heaven will be greater than the happiness and glory of those who have no such passions to contend with, and for whom virtue is so easy. God is just. He rewards each one according to his merits, that is to say, his combats and his victories. Oh! how agreeable to the Lord is the child, the young man, with great passions, who remains virtuous by the force of combats against his own heart, and victories against himself! You are already that child, my tender friend, and I foresee that you will be that young man. Great, too, will be your reward in Heaven, and beautiful will be your crown of glory in eternity.

Come again, my child, on the last day of the year, and, before I take my farewell of you, I shall tell you other means you can employ to conquer your passions in speaking to you of perseverance.

Your farewell, Father? Will that be the last time I shall come to see you?

Yes, my child, the last time.

Oh! Father, you make me sad. Adieu! dear good Father, pray for me, because, when I can no longer come to see you, what will become of me?

You will always have your Confessor, my child, and the Blessed Virgin! do you forget her? and your Angel Guardian and God! and the grace of Jesus-Christ! Have confidence, then, my child; place always your principal hope in *God alone.* The ministers of His word whom He will send to guide you from time to time during your life, He may leave with you or He may remove, according to His good pleasure and His designs upon you.

The beautiful Feast of Christmas, that is to say, the birthday of Our Lord Jesus-Christ, will occur on the 25th of this month. Celebrate that great Feast, not only this year but every year of your life, by approaching the Sacraments. If you have the happiness of assisting at Midnight Mass represent to yourself at that solemn hour a God becoming incarnate for love of you. Behold Him on His lowly pallet of straw, His little hands outstretched as if to give you His blessing. Admire his charity, His humility, His poverty. It is for you He suffers the inclemency of the season, the neglect of His own creatures. Pay Him your homage of adoration, love and gratitude. Supplicate His Virgin Mother to obtain for you the virtues that signalized His divine childhood. Salute also respectfully St. Joseph, her virginal spouse, and ask his intercession to obtain the graces of an interior spirit and a happy death.

Glory, all Glory, to God the Most High.

" The seraphim host from the heavens are singing,
  " Glory, all glory, to God the Most High!"
The echoes are catching, repeating and ringing,
  Glory, all glory, to God the Most High!"

Peal, Peal, the great bell from yon tower is vibrating,
  Mark, mark, how the faithful are wending along!
In the temple afar a Redeemer is waiting,
  And Bethlehem's angel repeateth his song!

As we enter the temple, the organ is pealing,
  The acolytes move and the choristers sing,
Sweet, solemn, the notes' round the altar are stealing,
  The smoke-wreathing censers the thurifers swing.

In his white robes of beauty the pontiff is praying,—
  Bright jewels the mitre and vestments adorn,—
And grand are the Masses the pontiff is saying,
  The Mass of the midnight, the Mass of the morn!

In thousands the faithful are kneeling around him,
  And thousands the eyes that are dim in their tears,
They seek for the Child, in the manger they found Him,
  Like an Infant of mercy sweet Jesus appears.

In the vault of the temple, the angel harp ringing,
  Glory, all glory, to God the Most High!
The organ is pealing, the choristers singing,
  Glory, all glory, to God the Most High.

J. K. F.

Let the last day of the year be for you a day of retreat or at least of recollection; read over your little memorandum, and see how you have passed the year of your FIRST COMMUNION. Now, promise me, my dear child, to be faithful to those recommendations which I have given you.

Yes, Father, *with the grace of God*, I shall be faithful.

Very well, my child, I see that during the last month you have learned to distrust yourself, and that you have not forgotten the advice I gave you on presumption and to place your strength in God alone. Continue, with all humility, to put your whole confidence in Him, and your perseverance will be certain. Go now, in peace, dear child, and pray for me.

THE LAST DAY OF THE YEAR.

31st of December.

FATHER, I come to see you, but quite sorrowful in the thought that it is for the last time.

Alas! that is so, my child, for we have arrived at the last day of the old year, and that year, so dear to your heart, the year of your First Communion. Thus it is that all things here below have an end, the days, the months, the years, and even life itself. We have not here a lasting city, but we seek one that is to come. In this world we are not citizens, but only passengers on our way to eternity. My child, would not that traveller be guilty of great folly who would consume all his wealth in building himself a dwelling in a place which he must soon leave?

Yes, Father. Then my child, I will exact from you another promise. Oh ! with all my heart, Father. What is it? It is my child, that next year you will unite with those who are preparing for their First Communion, in the retreat, and thus prepare to receive your second solemn Communion. I promise you, Father, but you said you would tell me other means of perseverance in the service of God. That is so, my child, I had almost forgotten, but I have a great many other things to tell you before our final separation. However, listen to these :

Means of Perseverance.

In our last two entertaiments on the critical age of youth and the combat of the passions, I

pointed out to you several means of perseverance. There remain a few more to add : 1st
To fly from the occasions of sin. Avoid, my
child, all bad company, for very soon such
would lead you to evil; 2nd. *To be devout to
the Blessed Virgin.* I have always remarked
that they who persevere in grace after their
First Communion are the faithful children of
Mary, and they, on the contrary, who abandon
God, begin by forsaking His Mother. Do not
forget that you consecrated yourself to that
Blessed and glorious Virgin on the day of your
First Communion, and be always faithful to
your practises of piety in her honor. 3rd. *The
frequentation of Sacraments.* It is im-
possible to persevere in virtue, my child, without those powerful aids, those sources of grace
which Jesus Christ himself has given us to
sustain our weakness. Continue to confess
and communicate as you have done since your
First Communion, and you will persevere in
virtue. 4th. *Spiritual reading.* Many children lose their souls after having received
their FIRST COMMUNION with much piety, and
their misfortune may be attributed to bad
books. On the contrary, those who persevere

in virtue, and thank God they are many, are assisted greatly by the reading of good books. If you have not access to a good Catholic library, ask your parents to procure you some good books, such as Catechism of Perseverance, Following of Christ, Spiritual Combat, and, Lives of the Saints ; instead of unnecessary expenses use your pocket money for the same laudable purpose. These will improve your mind, and give edification to your family. 5th. In fine, the great secret of perseverance is, not to be surprised at our falls, and not to be discouraged after a fault, rarely is a soldier victorious without having received some wound. If, then, my child, you commit faults, and you may expect to commit some, be not discouraged, but rise at once, and make an humble confession as you did last month after that unhappy fall which made you shed so many tears. Oh! my child, what comfort you gave me by your prompt conversion, it is to me the best warrant that you will persevere in the straight and narrow path leading to your heavenly home.

THE LAST WILL AND SPIRITUAL TESTAMENT OF THE ANGEL GUIDE.

Now, my child, before taking a final leave of you and bidding you a last farewell ere death closes my eyes to everything earthly, let me assure you that it is without regret that I leave this world of sin, this land of sorrow, of anxiety and care. Therefore, be not disheartened that I go. Heaven has designed that I must depart. My Father in His love calls me Home, but on the shores of eternity I hope through the mercy of God to see you again. Oh, Divine Lord! I accept death in whatever way Thou dost send it to me, and I beseech Thee to take pity upon one who has always desired to be Thy devoted servant.

Listen, my child, to my Last Will and Spiritual Testament, the last admonition I shall ever give you, for the voice of God speaks once more through me, His unworthy messenger. Love God with all your heart, He is your first beginning and your last end. He, the joy of your childhood, will be the hope of your youth, the consolation of your old age, and the reward of your eternity. Love also His blessed Mother. I leave you under her protection. My

last request is that you will pray for me when
I am dead, and I shall not forget you in that
land of the living, the home of the blessed.

When thou shalt kneel at Mary's shrine,
  And our dear Mother smiles on thee,
Forget not this request of mine,
  Oh! ask her then to pray for me.

And at the altar, when our Lord
  Shall deign to come and visit thee,
When thy devotion's finest chord
  Is touched by Him, then pray for me.

Oh sweet Communion! who can tell
  What glorious visions thou mayst see,
When Jesus in thy soul doth dwell?
  In that blest union, pray for me.

Beloved child, the wishes of my heart for
you are numerous and ardent. I began this
year by wishing you a worthy FIRST COM-
MUNION ; I now terminate it, praying that you
may persevere in the grace of God, next year,
and every year of your life. Oh! treasure
up in your soul the advices I have given you,
they will assist you in the battle of life, and
make you victorious in the struggle with the
enemy of light. The undying love of a
Merciful Redeemer will compensate you for the
weariness or loneliness of a life of labor to
which we are all condemned, and for the fickle-

ness and hollowness of earthly friendships.
Oh ! child of benediction, I wish you again,
during all your life the graces of the Lord,
final perseverance, a happy death, a glorious
resurrection, Heaven, God Himself, for all
eternity. Farewell, then, dear child, receive
the last blessing which I now give you with
my whole heart.

August 1st, 1879.

JESUS.

I need Thee, precious Jesus,
 I need a friend like Thee ;
A friend to soothe and sympathize,
 A friend to care for me.

I need Thy Heart, sweet Jesus,
 To feel each anxious care ;
I long to tell my every want,
 And all my sorrows share.

I need Thy Blood, sweet Jesus,
 To wash each sinful stain ;
To cleanse this sinful soul of mine
 And make it pure again.

I need Thy Wounds, sweet Jesus,
 To fly from perils near,
To shelter in those hallowed clefts,
 From every doubt and fear.

I need Thee, sweetest Jesus,
   In thy sacrament of Love ;
To nourish this poor soul of mine,
   With the treasures of Thy Love.

I'll need Thee, sweetest Jesus,
   When death's dread hour draws nigh,
To hide me in Thy Sacred Heart,
   Till wafted safe on high.

CONTENTS.

DEDICATION.

Picture of Angel Guardian and Child.
Poetry on the Angel Guardian.
JAN. 1st, 1880.—New Year's Wishes.

PAGE.

Invocations for First Communion, to obtain
    the grace to receive worthily 9
Essential preparation, the study of one's self.. 10
Child led by degrees to the knowlege of self.. 12
Angel Guide recommends certain practices... 14
JAN. 15th.—Studying to know one's self more and
    more 15
Goodness of heart tested 18
FEB. 1st.—New examination..................... 20
Advice on the 6th Commandment............ 25
Important admonition 27
Feb. 15th.—New and great things.............. 28
Child becomes a philosopher.............. 33
MARCH 1st.—Daily prayer to be used in prepara-
    tion for First Communion.................. 35
Recommendations 36
MARCH 2nd.—Third preparation for First Commu-
    nion—Religious Instruction 38
MARCH 8th.—Reformation of defects and acquiring
    of virtues insisted on 43
APRIL. 8th.—Sickness of child 47
New practices............................. 48

APRIL 12th.—Trial of child's disposition 49
Temptations 50
How to combat the temptations of the devil... 51
MAY.—Advices and daily prayer for the Month of
Mary................................. 54
Recommendation...................... 55
MAY 2nd.—Child received for First Communion... 56
General Confession.................... 57
Method of examination for same............ "
Prayer before Examination of Conscience..... "
First week of Entertainment
General Confession—I. Commandment...... 59
Important advice........................ 60
II. Commandment of God........ 61
III. Commandment of God, including 1st Pre-
cept of the Church................ 63
Second week of Instructions for the General
Confession 64
IV. Commandment of God................ "
V. Commandment of God................ 65
Particular note on this Commandment....... 66
VI. Commandment of God................ "
Particular note on this Commandment....... 67
Third week of Instruction for General Confes-
sion 68
VII. and X. Commandments of God........ "
Remarks particular to VII. Commandment... 69
VIII. Commandment of God...... .... "
Commandments or Precepts of the Church.... 70
Second Commandment of the Church........ "
Third Commandment of the Church, with
note................................. 71
Fourth Commandment of Church............ 72
Fifth Commandment of the Church.......... "

Sixth Commandment of the Church........ ..   73

Fourth week of Instruction of the General
    Confession........ ....   "

Capital Sins........   74

Duties of the State of Life......   75

Prayer for the First Communicant to excite
    Contrition   76

Prayer before Confession......   77

Advice and Method for Confession...........   78

Prayer after Confession .... ·.···..........   80

Advice........   81

MAY 12th.—First Return of the Child..........   82

MAY 15th.—Second Return of the Child...   84

MAY 25th.—Third Return of the Child..........   86

Reasons why a child may be kept back......,   "

JUNE 1st.—Month of the First Communion   87

Retreat of Three Days before the First Com-
    munion   90

Intentions of the Retreat......   91

Important Advice...... ....· ....   "

Exterior preparation......   92

First General Absolution............   93

How necessary to receive it well............   94

Pardon of Parents.........   95

Prayer of Child before going to receive General
    Absolution   96

Prayer after General Absolution ....   "

Essential Remarks for the morning of First
    Communion....   98

Souvenir of First Communion...... ....   "

The Great and Solemn Day, the Day of my
    First Communion......   99

Afternoon—Dialogue between Angel Guide and
    Child....   101

Renewal of Baptismal vows 104
Of Consecration to the Blessed Virgin 105
Act of Consecration 106
Day after First Communion 10
Mass of Thanksgiving .... "
Distribution of Prizes 109
Memorandum of eight pages 110
Memorandum Book 112
JULY 1st.—On the Fourth Sacrament to be received 118
AUGUST 1st.—Of the Second Communion......... 120
SEPTEMBER 1st.—Fervor and Exactitude recom-
mended 122
Catechism of Perseverance 123
Communion more or less frequent........... 124
OCTOBER 1st.—Child's conduct examined........ 126
Choice of a State of Life........ 128
Means of knowing the State of Life to which
God calls................................ 130
NOVEMBER 1st,—Praying for the dead............ 133
NOVEMBER 23rd.—Sorrowful return of the Child... 136
DECEMBER 1st.—Advent....................... 140
Youth is a critical and stormy age........... 141
DECEMBER 12th.—Spiritual Combat.............. 145
The Feast of Christmas....   150
Hymn, Glory, all glory to God the Most High. 151
Last day of the Year—Means of perseverance.. 152
Last Will and Testament of the Angel Guide.. 156
JESUS................................... 159

www.ingramcontent.com/pod-product-compliance
Lightning Source LLC
Chambersburg PA
CBHW031438280326
41927CB00038B/745